TOWARD WISER PUBLIC JUDGMENT

For Barbara

Dan Yankelovich

Toward Wiser Public Judgment

Daniel Yankelovich and
Will Friedman, Editors

Vanderbilt University Press

NASHVILLE

© 2010 by Public Agenda
Published by Vanderbilt University Press
Nashville, Tennessee 37235
First printing 2010

This book is printed on acid-free paper made
from 30% post-consumer recycled content.
Manufactured in the United States of America

Library of Congress Cataloging-in-Publication Data

Toward wiser public judgment / Daniel Yankelovich
and Will Friedman, editors.
p. cm.
ISBN 978-0-8265-1738-8 (cloth edition : alk. paper)
ISBN 978-0-8265-1739-5 (pbk. edition : alk. paper)
1. Political participation—United States.
2. Public opinion—United States.
3. Education—United States.
4. Educational change—United States.
I. Yankelovich, Daniel. II. Friedman, Will.
JK1764.T69 2010
323'.042—dc22
2010020353

Contents

Foreword

In fields ranging from technology, medicine, and science to business, communication, and culture, we see dynamic and rapid change. Nevertheless, in the midst of such promise and ingenuity, we reach the end of the first decade of the twenty-first century facing a growing number of troubling and systemic issues that we have come to label as "intractable." To name three in the United States, the long-term effectiveness and sustainability of our educational systems, our health and health care systems, and even our economic and financial systems are matters of grave concern.

As stewards of financial fortunes devoted to making things better, private foundations are encouraged to look for the root causes that underlie the conditions we seek to ameliorate. As a key source of funding our society's pluralistic research and development agenda, we look for opportunities where our financial investments can spur innovation, usually targeting the capacity of civil society to experiment with new approaches to solving social and economic problems. In *Toward Wiser Public Judgment*, the authors present a straightforward case: that our most difficult common problems will only become manageable when we turn our powers of reinvention on the *public problem-solving process* itself.

We can begin by framing the central contemporary question of our politics not by using the familiar dichotomy of *rights versus responsibilities*, but by asking what *skills* and *settings* best enable us to make hard collective choices. Put another way, embracing the value of helping people help themselves in more than individual or familial contexts, how do we increase the capacity of groups of democratic actors to tackle intractable problems, come to shared and deeply held judgments, and make hard choices that reflect the common good? This book not only provides insights and analysis but also reports on more than two decades of the practical application of "next-generation" approaches that show great promise in fostering wiser and more enduring public judgments.

The call to support more civic entrepreneurs in their efforts to create the conditions and opportunities for ordinary people to reengage in the critical work of democratic deliberation speaks forcefully to several critical issues of our day. With growing concern over the fate of newspapers and journalism, this book establishes a deeper context for the role information plays in the formation of public judgment. With increasing concern over the role and performance of our elected officials at local, state, and national levels, it defines effective leadership anew, demonstrating how empowered leaders play an essential role in the formation of public judgment.

A recent newspaper headline sums up the crisis of democracy that we face today: "Mood of the voters—all outrage, no action."[1] Outrage without action leads only to resentment and a susceptibility to quick fixes that never truly resolve complex, long-standing problems. We need a fresh approach. The American philosopher John Dewey said that "democracy has to be born anew every generation," and he regarded the essence of democracy as how a community collectively learns, how it generates and uses something he called social intelligence. *Toward Wiser Public Judgment* shows how the process of coming to public judgment can confront head-on the all too natural inclination we have for wishful thinking and easy answers. What's missing are new approaches to deliberation and dialogue focusing on values and choices, and taking seriously how individuals—ordinary people in a democracy—have socially, emotionally, cognitively, and historically solved their collective problems.

Those of us who focus most of our efforts on supporting the voluntary actions and associations of the nonprofit, independent sector often cite the observations of the French statesman Alexis de Tocqueville, who in the nineteenth century marveled at the ability of Americans to form voluntary associations in the sphere of private, civil society. What we must also remember is Tocqueville's insight that this capacity to organize—and the skills, trust, and experiences that enable and produce this capacity—are all derived from a politics that results in real public problem solving. The genius he observed was that what Americans learn from politics, they take to all the associations of civic life. "It is within political associations," Tocqueville observed, "that Americans of all conditions, of all minds, and of all ages get the general taste for association daily and familiarize themselves with its use." The result is a society of joiners and active citizens: "There [in political associations] they see each other in great number, speak to each other, understand each other, and in common become animated for all sorts of undertakings. Afterwards, they carry into civil life the notions they have acquired and make them serve a thousand uses."[2]

Toward Wiser Public Judgment is a call to action for a renewal of the authentic and effective public engagement essential to making sound public choices and public policies in the critical years before us.

Sterling Speirn, President
The W. K. Kellogg Foundation

Acknowledgments

This book is a project of Public Agenda's Center for Advances in Public Engagement (CAPE), and we would like to acknowledge the funders that have made the establishment of CAPE, and this work in particular, possible: the W. K. Kellogg Foundation and the Rockefeller Brothers Fund. We also express our appreciation to the excellent suggestions offered throughout the project by Michael Ames, our editor at Vanderbilt University Press, as well as to two excellent reviewers who gave the manuscript exceptionally careful and thoughtful readings and offered comments, questions, and challenges that decidedly improved the final product.

Additionally, Dan Yankelovich would like to acknowledge the stimulation and inspiration of collaborating with his colleagues at the Public Agenda, the Kettering Foundation, and Viewpoint Learning, Inc.

Will Friedman would like to acknowledge his frequent collaborator, Alison Kadlec, director of CAPE, whose sharp intellect, scholarly commitment, and delight in challenging sacred cows have made him a better thinker; his many wonderful and hard-working colleagues at Public Agenda; and his family, Kathleen, Nick, and Hallie: endlessly supportive, wonderfully diverting.

TOWARD WISER PUBLIC JUDGMENT

How Americans Make Up Their Minds

The Dynamics of the Public's Learning Curve
and Its Meaning for American Public Life

Daniel Yankelovich and Will Friedman

The purpose of this book is to bring up to date the findings and insights of Daniel Yankelovich's *Coming to Public Judgment*, which was published in 1991.[1] That work confronted a subject that our society (as well as most practitioners in the field of public opinion) prefers to ignore, namely, the *quality* of American public opinion. In this context *high-quality* opinion does not mean opinion that agrees with experts' views; instead it means opinion that is stable and coherent and that takes consequences into account. Practitioners have been so preoccupied with the difficult task of *measuring* public opinion that they have brushed aside the question of whether the opinions they are measuring in their polls reflect thoughtful public judgment on vital issues, or mindless venting, or something in between.

Coming to Public Judgment argued that people advance through several distinctively different stages before they form politically meaningful judgments about public issues. Most notably, people must "work through" the temptation to opt for easy answers and wishful thinking. They must often reconcile conflicting sets of values. And they must come to terms with some tough trade-offs before they can truly accept and support any new course of action. The difference between "raw" public opinion and public opinion that has been worked through in this fashion is the difference between carefully considered judgments and fickle opinion that changes on a dime—or as a result of the latest clever "partisan framing" of a problem.

Genuine public judgment is often the result of considerable effort extending over years and sometimes decades. People require time and hard work to come to terms with the realities of an issue—a "working-through" process in which they gradually assimilate the consequences of various paths of action. We have dedicated many years of research to mapping the typical "learning curve" that citizens follow when struggling with difficult issues. When the learning curve on any one issue is successfully completed, it provides a stable foundation of public support consonant with core American values.

Three Overall Conclusions

Between us, we bring seven decades of experience to conducting empirical investigations of how Americans make up their minds on important public issues. Our work has employed a variety of methods, including public opinion polls, focus groups, case histories, trend-tracking studies, longitudinal studies, various dialogue methods, and community forums. We can summarize what we have learned from this vast array of data under three headings.

1. The media base their reporting on a set of assumptions that bear almost no resemblance to the way people actually make up their minds.

Dan Yankelovich's chapter, immediately following this introduction, elaborates this point at length. Essentially, the media assume that factual information is the key to thoughtful public judgment: give the public the facts, and once people receive the relevant information they will make up their own minds. This picture has immense rational appeal, but unfortunately it happens not to be valid. The public's learning curve is an immensely complex process, with factual information often playing a limited, even minor role in advancing it.

One implication of this reality is that public opinion polls are often badly misleading. When people criticize opinion polls, they usually point to technical problems such as badly worded questions or skewed samples. But when polls are misleading, the reason is less likely to be a technical flaw in the polling than the fact that people haven't made up their minds about the issue being polled, whether it is health care, immigration, education, or reforming Wall Street. And when people haven't made up their minds, their answers to poll questions are unreliable and wander all over the place.

2. *Since* Coming to Public Judgment *was published in the early 1990s, we and other research and citizen engagement practitioners have developed promising new methods for helping people make up their minds on complex, difficult issues.*

These new methods are described in a number of the chapters that follow. The new methods all follow the logic of the public's learning curve. Once we were able to establish that the public's learning curve evolves through a series of stages, we began to devise methods for helping people advance through the various stages in an accelerated form.

The new methods, many of them dialogue based, potentially provide an indispensable tool for today's political and civic leadership. This is because so many of today's important issues suffer from a *time-gap* problem, by which we mean that the time required for the public to come to sound judgment on an issue is badly out of sync with the urgency of the need for timely solutions. Our nation cannot afford to procrastinate and let these problems fester unresolved.

Once our political and civic leaders understand the logic of the public's learning curve on any issue, they have in hand a powerful tool for helping the public overcome the kind of wishful thinking, quick-fix illusions, value conflicts, and misunderstandings that can bog issues down for years, if not decades.

3. *Our political culture resonates with the public's desire for a stronger voice, but it badly underestimates the importance of ensuring that this voice reflects sound public judgment and not raw, mindless emotion.*

Our culture's reluctance to confront the issue of ensuring that the public voice reflects sound judgment continues unabated. Most practitioners of public opinion research do not regard the quality of public opinion as their concern. And most political leaders assume that they must treat public opinion as a sacred object, however poor its quality may be, as if no special effort were required to ensure that the public genuinely understands the issues and has formed thoughtful responses to them.

As a consequence, vast amounts of energy are devoted to mobilizing public opinion, with very little effort devoted to enhancing the quality of public judgment. The media, whose efforts to achieve this objective are indispensable, think they are doing their job while continuing to adhere to an outmoded journalistic ideology. Elites are more concerned about their own power and influence than about the quality of public judgment. And academic institutions remain mostly oblivious.

This problem can jeopardize the future of our democracy; it cries out for careful and considered concern.

Our Shifting Culture

The years between the earlier book and now have changed American society in a number of ways that bear directly on the central themes of this book. The advent of the Internet and the subsequent weakening of traditional news media are among the important new conditions that affect how citizens engage issues. So are the continued growth of skepticism toward government authority among Americans, today's sharp political polarization, and the decline in the civility of our political discourse.

These changes present new challenges to the cause of helping the public come to terms with the complex issues we face—and these have, if anything, gotten more difficult to deal with since *Coming to Public Judgment* was published. As we write, our nation confronts an intimidating set of challenges, as profound and dire as any since the 1930s: a near-cataclysmic economic collapse atop an unsustainable budget deficit, an insecure energy future, a dangerously vulnerable natural environment, unstable relationships with a number of Muslim countries, threats of terrorism, uncontrolled nuclear proliferation, pandemics, and so on. It is a sobering list of high-stakes tests of our nation's ability to cope with complex problems.

What will it take to ensure that our democracy is up to the task of addressing these large "time-gap" issues? Under today's conditions, citizens have little chance to grasp the full complexity of issues of this sort and to wrestle with the trade-offs and sacrifices they may require. We know from decades of research with the public that prevailing conditions are not set in stone, and that citizens can, when provided with the *right* conditions, come to terms with critical issues in a timely fashion and in democratically meaningful ways.

How to create the conditions for a more thoughtful and effective public voice is our major focus in this book. In a democracy, the public voice is often decisive—sometimes in a positive sense, but also in the negative sense that the public can exercise a practical veto that can undermine the best-laid plans of experts and leaders. Sound and sustainable policy must be based on a solid foundation of public judgment.

Advancing the Public's Learning Curve

Coming to Public Judgment also explored what might be done to advance the working-through stages of the public's learning curve when it encounters the sorts of obstacles that can paralyze the public's learning curve for decades (e.g., health care reform).[2] The present volume continues this effort by examining Yankelovich's book in light of current events and drawing on several decades of theory and practice following its publication.[3] What have we learned since the book was published? What critical questions must we explore to narrow the gap so that the dire time-gap challenges we face may be more effectively met?

In one way or another, the essays in this book all speak to this last critical question and address the essential things that must be done to facilitate public judgment and leadership's capacity to take the public's perspectives fully into account. They show that it is indeed possible to help citizens confront and "work through" tough and complex issues, and that civil, problem-solving dialogue is possible even on emotionally charged topics. They also provide many examples of the ways in which processes that help citizens come to public judgment have had important impacts on public policy and community politics.

At a minimum, the various contributions herein suggest that the following three items are critical needs of a more public judgment–oriented politics.

1. More Effective Ways to Present Issues to the Public *values*

Many issues are laden with strong emotions and oblige the public to accept changes and make sacrifices. The rules for helping the public confront and work through emotional issues (and the time it takes for the public to absorb such issues) are vastly different from the rules governing the presentation and absorption of emotion-neutral facts.

The media often treat people as if they were attentive experts who can take in reams of data, rather than inattentive citizens with busy lives who are more interested in the *values* underlying policy choices and the *practical consequences* of action than they are in the technical side of things.

It is true that some parts of the media, such as talk radio and cable news, are values oriented in their presentations. But their messages suffer from different flaws. They are often partisan, polarized, and highly ideological. Issues are presented as if there are only two black-and-white possibilities, with little room for pragmatic compromise, practical innovations, or other points of view.

2. More Effective Ways to Brief Leaders on the Willingness of the Public to Confront Tough Choices

Leaders need a deeper understanding than they typically have of the public's evolving views and openness to change and sacrifice. They need to understand how citizens can come to responsible judgment rather than simply be the objects of "spin." They need to understand the public's starting point on issues, and how far along people are in their learning curve at any one point in time—e.g., have they just begun to think about an issue, or have they been doing so for a long time? Leaders need to be aware of the values, perceptions, and misperceptions the public brings to issues, and the state of their judgment about what is to be done. They need a sense of the direction that people take as they wrestle with issues more fully and effectively.

3. More Effective Ways to Help the Broad Public Move toward Judgment

Finally, our institutions need to develop more effective ways of helping citizens work through issues and move steadily along the learning curve. Presenting issues to the public more effectively, as discussed earlier, is only one part of the challenge; there are all sorts of ways in which public learning, dialogue, and deliberation can be organized and facilitated.

Fortunately, leadership has a wider array of tools to use for this purpose today than were available at the time *Coming to Public Judgment* was published. An entire movement is taking shape in academia, local government, and the nonprofit sector that is dedicated to developing the tools, strategies, and know-how to promote greater public understanding and engagement. And, in an unprecedented move, President Obama has called for greater and more innovative public engagement across the federal government.

Organization of the Book

The chapters in this book speak to these various ways of accelerating the public's learning curve. Chapter 1 offers reflections by Dan Yankelovich on his original theory of public judgment. He explores what has held up and what bears reformulating in light of current events and a broader base of experience and experimentation in helping the public learn about, and come to judgment on, critical public issues. Chapter 2 elaborates on these reflections in an interview of Yankelovich by his co-editor, Will Friedman.

The writers of the next three, applied chapters represent organizations or initiatives dedicated to enhancing the quality of public judgment: National Issues Forums, Public Agenda, and Viewpoint Learning, Inc. Certainly, the work of many other practitioners and organizations could have been included as well. We chose these three because they are each enterprises in which Yankelovich played a direct role and because they are the three efforts in the field that have struggled most directly and self-consciously with his ideas about public judgment. We believe that others have been influenced by the public judgment thesis to one extent or another, and certainly the work of many other organizations and initiatives is extremely relevant to the book's ideas and could have been fruitfully included. But we decided on the strategy of delving into those organizations that have intentionally incorporated a public judgment framework, albeit to different extents and in different ways, hoping that this would maintain a useful and clear focus on the ideas at the heart of the book.

Collectively, these organizations have more than seventy years of "on-the-ground" experience in creating conditions that help citizens engage issues effectively. In Chapter 3, Keith Melville and Bob Kingston describe the work of the National Issues Forums (NIF), the community-based, public deliberation network that the Kettering Foundation brought into being almost thirty years ago. In this chapter, the two authors (each of whom has been involved with NIF from the beginning) reflect on what they have learned about the public's coming to judgment as a result of observing hundreds of public forum deliberations on scores of topics.

Alison Kadlec and Will Friedman in Chapter 4 describe how Public Agenda combines public opinion research and public engagement strategies to help citizens come to judgment on a wide variety of issues. They reflect on how Public Agenda's evolution relates to Yankelovich's conceptualizations in *Coming to Public Judgment*.

Steve Rosell and Heidi Gantwerk, representing the work of Viewpoint Learning, Inc., end this part of the book. In Chapter 5, they describe Viewpoint Learning's research strategies to replicate the public's process of coming to judgment through carefully constructed, eight-hour experimental dialogues with small cross sections of the public. This work starts where Yankelovich's critique in *Coming to Public Judgment* of traditional public opinion polling left off, by attempting to go "beyond surveys and focus groups." Their research gives leaders an indication of the future shape of public judgment after the public has had an opportunity to work through the pros and cons of issues.[4]

After these three applied chapters, Will Friedman concludes by reflecting on what he considers the two cutting-edge questions of "public judgment politics" and the larger field of deliberative democratic work: How can we strengthen the impacts on policy making and other forms of public problem solving of efforts to help citizens come to public judgment? And how can this work, which has been manifested most strongly on the local level, become more central and meaningful to national politics? The latter question is examined with special attention to the opportunities and potential pitfalls that the Obama administration presents.

PART I

THE CONCEPT OF PUBLIC JUDGMENT

CHAPTER I

How to Achieve
Sounder Public Judgment

DANIEL YANKELOVICH

My conclusion in *Coming to Public Judgment* in the early 1990s was that American public opinion on most issues of the day did not meet the high standards of sound judgment necessary to make our democracy flourish as it should. The problem was not due to public ignorance or prejudice or ideological polarization. On the contrary, in the decades I have spent monitoring and analyzing American public opinion, my regard for American pragmatism and practicality has only increased. I approached the quality problem from the perspective of someone with deep respect for the public voice.

The main flaw in public opinion discussed in the earlier book derived from a badly distorted and misleading model of public opinion that dominated—and still dominates—the expert culture of our society, including journalists, scientists, business leaders, scholars, professional experts, and political leaders.

Our research with the public suggested that the institutions of our society charged with shaping public opinion operate under a set of false assumptions about the forces that mold public opinion and how public opinion evolves over time. As a result, these institutions do a poor job of preparing Americans to cope with the problems that threaten to overwhelm us. The media go for overkill in alerting the public to potential train wrecks, while offering very little help in averting them or preparing us to cope with them constructively. Political leaders find it easier to pander to the most intensely felt convictions of the public than to present real choices for public consideration. Scientists labor under the illusion that if only we could improve the public's science literacy, the nation would arrive at sensible solutions to problems.

These misunderstandings of American public opinion on the part of leaders caused the quality of public judgment to suffer two decades ago, when the earlier book was published. The events of recent years have made the problem even more severe and urgent. Elites have grown even more ideologically driven and polarized, and they transmit their divisive attitudes to the larger public.

In this chapter, I want to accomplish two tasks. The first is to redescribe the thesis of the 1991 book within a framework I did not use in the earlier book. The new framework is based on the concept of *the public's learning curve*—the process the public undertakes as it struggles to understand complex issues and how best to address them.

This learning curve concept helps communicate an essential aspect of how public opinion develops that is strikingly different from the dominant theory of public opinion formation. The prevailing theory sees public opinion formation as a simple *transaction*: the media provide their audiences with information that is absorbed as it is transmitted; its content is wholly cognitive; I may react emotionally to it, in anger or disgust or with eager enthusiasm. But the transaction itself is assumed to be a simple, direct matter of communicating facts, ideas, and opinion, conveyed and absorbed simultaneously.

Those of us engaged in studying public opinion have learned from thousands of surveys and analyses that this model of public opinion formation could hardly be more false and misleading. Public opinion formation is, in fact, not a single transaction but a multistage *process* that takes place over weeks, months, years, even decades. On emotion-laden issues, it is analogous to something like the grief process, as the grieving person shifts from one stage to another—evolving step by step from, for example, denial to depression to anger to sorrow and ultimately to acceptance. So, too, on difficult and complex issues (the housing crisis, for example), public opinion evolves though a series of stages, starting with consciousness raising and advancing though a growing sense of urgency mixed with skepticism, denial, wishful thinking, anger, blame, and mistrust, and eventually to acceptance and practical decision making.

The image of an arduous learning curve that the public climbs with more or less difficulty evokes this multistage process. In Part 1 of this chapter, I reframe within the learning curve concept those findings of the 1991 book that have stood the test of time and remain valid under the different conditions of the present era of American life.

My second objective in this chapter is to identify the changes that have taken place in the intervening years that are strategically important in achieving sounder public judgment in America. Some of these changes make the quality problem more severe. Others hold the promise that significant improvements can be made in the way the American public reaches sound judgment on issues.

Part 2 of this chapter flags some of the new forces working *against* sounder public judgment. These include the following:

- the sharper political polarization of the country
- the mounting public mistrust of our institutions as they fail to cope with ever more overwhelming problems
- an erosion in the nation's traditional problem-solving capabilities
- a persistent gap between the nation's scientists and technical experts and the general public
- the public's insistence on having a stronger say in the decisions that affect people's lives, without recognizing what it takes to arrive at responsible judgments rather than deeply felt convictions
- the tendency of political leaders to pander to the worse prejudices of the public rather than to launch the sorts of discussions that lead to sounder public judgment

These forces can be seen in particularly sharp relief through the example of the deep divide between science and society.

Part 3 of the chapter elaborates some of the newer, more positive forces we can deploy to advance the quality of public judgment. Three are particularly noteworthy. One force is broader recognition of the need to engage the public through more deliberative forms of discussion and dialogue. Closely linked to this is the development of a variety of techniques for advancing the public's learning curve on vital issues. A third force—one that I deem to be of utmost importance—is more theoretical in character. It relates to the neuroscientific discovery that the traditional dichotomy between the cognitive and the emotional aspects of judgment is highly artificial and misleading.

Part 1. Toward a More Accurate Picture of Public Opinion

The dominant model of opinion formation, as the media and many experts conceive it, is a top-down structure in which experts, leaders, journalists, bloggers, and even entertainers transmit information to the public, who simultaneously absorb it and arrive at considered judgment. One refinement

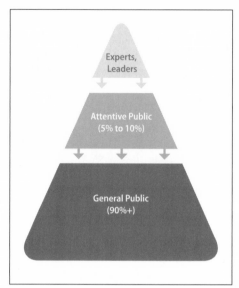

Figure 1.1

has expert opinion transmitted to the general public through the intermediary of the so-called attentive public (sometimes called "thought leaders" or "influentials"). The dominant model looks like the one in Figure 1.1.

This model of public opinion formation is flawed in three ways.

Flaw #1: It Assumes That Information Is the Main Driver of the Public's Learning Curve

According to the model, "sound" public opinion equals "well-informed" opinion; by definition, those who are poorly informed have poor-quality opinions.

This idea goes back to Thomas Jefferson's famous dictum that democracy depends on "an informed citizenry." However, Jefferson used the term "informed" in its eighteenth-century Enlightenment sense—to include thoughtfulness, ethical soundness, and good judgment as well as factual information. Today's experts and journalists have hollowed out this thick meaning of being informed. They are more restrictive and more likely to equate being well informed with having a lot of factual information. This serious misunderstanding is reflected in Figure 1.2.

It would be perverse to deny that information is relevant to the quality of public opinion. Obviously, information plays some role in shaping public

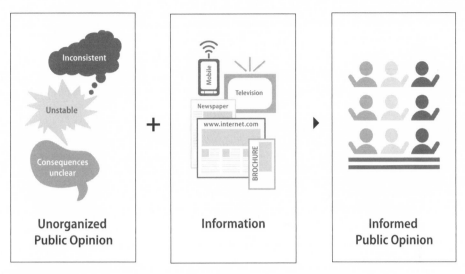

Figure 1.2

opinion. But public opinion research shows that it is often a secondary role. To assume that public opinion is invariably improved by inundating people with information grossly exaggerates the role of information and underestimates the importance of values and emotions.

Flaw #2: It Assumes That Expert Analysis and Debates between Experts Are Sound Ways to Shape Public Opinion

The media give a lot of attention to expert analysis and debate. In "expert analysis" leaders and experts make speeches, brief reporters, write op-ed pieces, and appear on talk shows often in debate format to convey their thinking and to share a tiny fraction of their knowledge with the public.

Serious news shows, for example, are filled with discussions and debates among experts in the economics and foreign policy fields. Often these programs have the opposite effect of what is intended. Instead of making people feel they understand the issues better, detailed expert talk confirms viewers' assumption that the discussion could not conceivably be aimed at them. Even experts sincerely committed to bringing the public into policy discussions will sometimes impede the process by insisting on correct terminology as the "price" of the public's participation. For example, experts concerned about the national debt may feel that the first order of business is to explain the difference between publicly held debt and trust fund debt. Although teaching people this distinction satisfies experts, it does little to help citizens resolve their conflicting desires to maintain government services while avoiding tax increases.

Even more misguided is the practice of having experts holding opposing views debate their positions. While such debates can be dramatic (a major reason the media rely on this format), these arguments do little to help the public along the learning curve. Unable to evaluate the arguments and wary of being misled by one side or the other, most members of the public turn away in frustration, grumbling, "If even the experts can't agree, how can we decide?"

In addition, these messages are not actually absorbed by the public in real time. It takes a long time for stable public opinion to form on complex issues—much longer than the time needed for the media to convey information and the public to absorb it. Instead of following a simple "information-in-judgment-out" process, the public mind evolves through a long and complex dynamic.

Flaw #3: It Assumes That the Media and Experts Are the Main Shapers of Public Opinion Because They Are the Key Sources of Factual Information

It is true that on most issues media coverage is indispensable to the first stage of the learning curve—consciousness raising. Typically, the public begins its learning curve journey with inconsistent and unstable views whose consequences are not well understood. As the public advances along the learning curve on an issue, its views become more stable, less contradictory, and more consistent. But the later stages of the learning curve are rarely driven by media-based information. Instead, they are fundamentally *social* processes. They advance if and when people talk the issue over with one another—family members, coworkers, neighbors, and friends.

Figure 1.3 shows a more accurate model of public opinion formation. Information has a role to play, but rarely the most important one. The key dynamic in public opinion formation is an emotion-laden, value-driven, time-consuming process of overcoming our natural inclination to denial and wishful thinking over extended periods of time.

Toward a More Accurate Picture of Public Opinion

Here now is a brief inventory of our key research findings about public opinion formation that have stood the test of time since *Coming to Public Judg-*

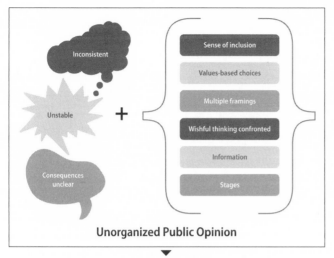

Unorganized Public Opinion

Sound Public Judgment

Figure 1.3

ment was published. They remain valid under the different conditions of the present era of American life.

1. The time required for people to come to sound judgment on complex, emotion-laden issues depends on the issue and varies enormously. Some issues require only months to complete the learning curve to reach sound public judgment; other issues take decades or even centuries (e.g., slavery or women's rights).

2. On the nation's most urgent challenges, it sometimes takes longer than the time available for people to make up their minds, especially on is-

sues that involve painful trade-offs. On time-gap issues like global climate change and our dependence on foreign oil, this reality poses a serious obstacle to sound public policy decision making.

3. On issues involving trade-offs that create conflict, people need to go through a complex learning curve that involves several time-consuming stages of struggling with issues before they arrive at sound public judgment. Typically, the learning curve evolves through three distinct stages, each with its own substages:

- **Stage I: Consciousness raising**. In this first stage the public becomes aware of an issue and begins to take it seriously. This stage is largely media-driven, and news events are a major factor in expediting the process (e.g., four-dollar-per-gallon gasoline, Hurricane Katrina, the worst credit crisis since the 1930s, the Gulf of Mexico oil spill). Sometimes consciousness raising proceeds with agonizing slowness, but, unlike the next two stages, it can sometimes be accomplished with great speed.

- **Stage II: Working through**. *Consciousness raising* initiates a *"working-through"* stage in which the public begins to confront the need for change, considers the pros and cons of proposed actions, and wrestles with trade-offs. In this stage of the learning curve people struggle to reconcile their positions on issues with their core values. In this sometimes stormy process, emotions play a more prominent role than objective analysis and deliberation.

    This is the stage where issues most frequently bog down— sometimes for a very long time. As observers of human psychology know well, all change is difficult. People caught in cross pressures must overcome the temptation to fall back on denial and wishful thinking before they can resolve them. They must face and resolve the conflicts, ambivalences, and defenses the issues arouse. Rarely does the course of change proceed smoothly. It is full of backsliding and procrastination and avoidance. "Two steps forward and one step back" is an apt description of this process.

    Though events can sometimes affect the working-through process, they are not critical to it. Working through is a largely social process: individuals usually work problems through in discussion with others until they ultimately achieve resolution for themselves. Unlike consciousness raising, the working-through process is not media driven or information dependent. Generally, people engaged in working through may have all the information they need long before they are willing or able to confront the cross pressures that ensnare them. And finally, in contrast with the consciousness-raising stage, our society is not well equipped with the institutions or knowledge it needs to expedite working through tough issues. Our culture does not understand this process very well, and by and large does not do a good job with it. In brief, then, the wrenching discontinuity between the media/event-driven consciousness-raising phase and the working-through phase is a major source of difficulty in any effort to help the public advance along the learning curve.

- **Stage III: Resolution**. The third stage is resolution, in which the public completes the learning curve. People choose a course of action and are prepared to accept its likely consequences. In these final stages of the process, people sign on, having worked through both their emotional resistances and the cognitive weighing of pros and cons. Full resolution moves through two substages, as people advance from intellectual assent to a full commitment of both heart and mind. Empirical research shows that the cognitive aspects come first, while the moral and emotional aspects lag behind. People form a resolution first in their heads; it takes a while for their hearts and consciences to catch up.

4. Visualizing this three-stage process, one can imagine the public encountering a steep slope littered with obstacles (Fig. 1.4). There are many ways to the crest of this hill. The path can seem insurmountably steep, and it is easy to slide back down. But once people reach the summit—the top of the curve—the path forward becomes easier and clearer.

5. Each one of the three stages of this learning curve is subject to different forms of resistance—and each requires different institutions and rules of engagement to move the process along. While our society has excellent mechanisms for *consciousness raising* and *resolution* (Stages I and III), we are seriously lacking in institutions that can midwife the Stage II phase of *working through*.

6. If the public, for whatever reason, is unable to move through all three stages, then the learning curve is incomplete. When the public offhandedly rejects the need for tax increases to reduce the federal budget deficit on the grounds that correcting waste, fraud, and abuse would make the problem disappear, this is an incomplete learning curve. There may be sound reasons to oppose tax increases, but the ritualistic incantation of "waste, fraud, and abuse" serves merely as a rationalization that people seize on because it permits them to avoid confronting the real issue.

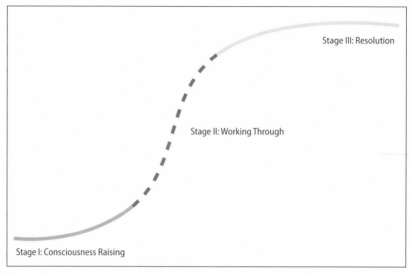

Figure 1.4

7. When the public has completed the learning curve on an issue, people's views are less likely to change when survey questions are worded differently or when the same question is asked weeks or months later. They remain constant even as events roll on. People have connected the dots and have moved beyond compartmentalized thinking. Their positions need not be ideologically pure or unswervingly logical, but they do reflect their core values. And most important of all, people fully grasp—and accept—the consequences of their views.

Part 2. Forces Working *against* Sound Public Judgment

Since *Coming to Public Judgment* was published in the early 1990s, a number of changes in the culture and society have exacerbated the quality problem and added to our flawed processes of reaching public judgment.

Proliferation of "Time-Lag" Problems
Perhaps the most obvious and important of these changes is the mounting number of overwhelming problems that the nation is obliged to confront and deal with effectively. These include the following:

[handwritten marginal note:] how to complete learning curve on local issues

- a major financial crisis
- staggering national debt, swelling as the nation ages
- global warming exacerbated by U.S. and China policies
- unprecedented transfer of wealth to pay for the oil imported from nations hostile to our interests
- severe loss of U.S. standing in the world
- a poorly understood—and dangerous—conflict with the Muslim world
- rising costs of health care and higher education that threaten the social contract

All these problems require thoughtful public input, and we don't have the luxury of time to figure out what to do about them. These are "time-lag" problems—so urgent that the lag in the public's normal learning curve may compromise an effective response. This is why we need new methods of accelerating public opinion formation. We need to find new ways to have the American public participate in solving our nation's most pressing problems in a timely fashion.

So far we have been lucky: we have muddled through without irreparable damage to our society and our world. But our margin of error is growing ever narrower and the risks of just muddling through more harmful and destructive.

The tempo of events has increased, and their effects are felt on a much larger scale. This means that the public has less time to come to grips with major changes, and in our interconnected world the consequences affect far more people far more quickly. This increased tempo and consequence of events gives leaders less time to help the public climb the learning curve before the next crisis erupts.

To make matters worse, people are drowning in conflicting information. Not only can it be difficult for leaders to compete with all the myriad sources available; the explosion of sources allows people to self-select which forms of information are most congenial to them. Most will choose those that mesh with their existing perspectives. In the current media landscape it is simply harder to reach those who do not already agree with you.

Intensity of Conviction as a Substitute for Sound Judgment

The time-lag problem and other negative influences appear to be eroding our national gift for pragmatic problem solving. We see evidence of this erosion all around us. For more than three decades we have been talking about school reform without essentially doing anything about it. Vast numbers of baby boomers are about to retire, placing unbearable financial strains on Medicare that we are ignoring at the peril of younger generations. We permitted an unsustainable housing bubble to reach the point where its bursting has put the entire economy in jeopardy. In testimony before Congress, former Federal Reserve Chairman Alan Greenspan admitted shock at the failure of the financial community to protect its own long-term self-interest—a failure that Vanguard's John Bogle attributes to putting "salesmanship" ahead of "stewardship."[1]

Problems are proliferating, the nation is polarized, we are bogged down in a series of "culture wars," parts of our society appear to have lost their ethical bearings, and competing power centers are pulling the public in all sorts of different directions.

And in the midst of all this, the public is demanding an ever-stronger say for itself. On the surface, this insistence should be counted as a source of strength for our democracy. We are purportedly a government "of the people and by the people." But under today's conditions (as we discussed in the Introduction), it is instead a source of weakness. This is largely because we have failed to recognize that a stronger public voice must be conditioned on the public's accepting full responsibility for the soundness and consequences of its views.

This position is fundamental to the central thesis of *Coming to Public Judgment*. There is a minimum level of *quality* of public opinion needed to give public opinion the *gravitas* required to shape sound pragmatic solutions to serious problems. The public can be said to have completed the learning curve when the following occurs:

1. People's views reach stability and become firm.
2. People's views are free from internal contradictions and disconnects.
3. People accept responsibility for the consequences of their views.

All three of these structural characteristics of public opinion are readily measurable in conventional opinion polls (though they are, in fact, rarely measured). The most important of the three dimensions of quality is the third: accepting responsibility for the consequences of your views. Do those who favor the death penalty appreciate the reality that given the fallibility of our legal system, innocent people may die? Do the strong supporters of ethanol for environmental reasons appreciate its huge impact on the price of food? Do those who think we should not meet unconditionally with the leaders of hostile nations appreciate the potential loss of making diplomatic headway?

For our democracy to work well, with a strong role for the public voice, the public must appreciate the potential consequences of its own views. This is surely one of the best definitions of sound judgment. It is when this element is lacking that we are most likely to confront the conditions that Yeats immortalized in "The Second Coming": "Things fall apart; the center cannot hold. . . . The best lack all conviction, while the worst are full of passionate intensity." There is, unfortunately, a widespread assumption in our culture that passionate intensity can substitute for sound judgment. In today's America, the evidence of the folly of that conviction is not hard to find.

The Great Divide: Science as a Case in Point

America's long tradition of individualism and participation in civic life has evolved in ways that are far more radical than they appear at first. The change began to take off with the dramatic shift in values that took place in the 1960s, when values of expressiveness, individualism, and freedom began to take priority over conformity and self-sacrifice. The greater value placed on individual agency and self-expression had enormous impact on our culture—spurring not only greater civil rights for women and minorities, increased pluralism, and reduced social conformity but also a dramatic expansion of whose voices "count" in public and political life.

In recent years, the public's willingness to accept the authority of experts and elites has sharply declined. Throughout most of our nation's history, leaders have held a quasi-monopoly on decision making; but recent changes in cultural values have led people to insist on having a stronger voice on issues that affect their lives. The public does not want to scrap representative democracy and move wholesale toward radical populism. But there will be no return to the earlier habits of deference to authority and elites.

What we have instead is a vast divide separating America's experts and elites from the general public and compromising our public judgment process. This divide is especially acute, and especially dangerous, when it comes to science. Science has reached greater heights of sophistication and productivity, while at the same time the gap between science and public life has grown ever larger—to an extent that now poses a serious threat to our future.

Increasingly critical problems at the intersection of science and society (such as the energy crisis, global climate change, and the danger posed by pandemic disease) are exacerbated by the growing gulf between scientists and the public. Such issues are even more critical and challenging today than when the 1991 book was published. They bring into stark relief the challenge of many complex contemporary issues for the public judgment process.

The unfortunate reality is that experts/scientists and the rest of society operate out of vastly different worldviews, especially in relation to assumptions about what constitutes knowledge and how to deal with it. Scientists share a worldview that presupposes rationality, lawfulness, and orderliness. They believe that answers to most empirical problems are ultimately obtainable if we pose the right questions and approach them scientifically. They are comfortable with measurement and quantification, and they take the long view. They believe in sharing information, and their orientation is internationalist because they know that discoveries transcend borders.

The nonscientific world of everyday life in the United States marches to a different drummer. Public life is shot through and through with irrationality, discontinuity, and disorder. Decision makers rarely have the luxury of waiting for verifiable answers to their questions, and when they do, they almost never go to the trouble and cost of developing them. Average Americans are uncomfortable with probabilities, especially in relation to risk assessment, and have short time horizons. Most problems are experienced with an urgency and immediacy that make people impatient for answers; policy makers must deal with issues as they arise and cannot ignore those that are difficult to address through rational analysis.

The media serve to deepen the divide with their insistence on presenting "both sides" of all stories that touch on scientific findings. In practice, this means that even when there is overwhelming consensus in the scientific community (as in the case of global warming), experts all too often find themselves pitted in the media against some contrarian, crank, or shill on hand to provide "proper balance" (and verbal fireworks). The resulting arguments actively hinder people's ability to reach sound understanding: not only do they muddy the public's already shaky grasp of scientific fundamentals, but they also leave people confused and disoriented.

When faced with the gap between science and society, scientists assume that the solution is to make the public more science literate, to do a better job at science education and so bring nonscientists around to a more scientific mind-set. This assumption conveniently absolves science of the need to examine the way its own practices contribute to the gap and allows science to maintain its position of intellectual and moral superiority. In addition, on a purely practical level, a superficial smattering of scientific knowledge might cause more problems than it solves.

The timetables of science (which operates in a framework of decades or longer) are completely out of sync with the timetables of public policy (which operates in a framework of months and years). For example, it has taken nearly thirty years for the National Academy of Sciences to complete its study of the consequences of oil drilling on Alaska's North Slope; in that time a great deal of environmental damage has been done, and political pressure for further oil exploration in the Arctic National Wildlife Refuge has gained momentum. At this stage the academy's scientific report stands to become little more than a political football. Medical research is another example. Political demands for prompt action on high-profile diseases do not jibe well with the painstaking process of research and trial. Political pressures push resources toward popular or expedient solutions, not necessarily those with the greatest chance of long-term success.

Nor are these the only symptoms. A host of other elements widen the gap between the two worlds: unresolved collisions with religious beliefs, difficulty in assessing the relative importance of threats, the growing number and complexity of issues. The overall result is a dangerous exclusion of the scientific viewpoint from political and economic decision making at the very time when that viewpoint is most urgently needed.

Part 3. Forces Working *for* Sound Judgment

Fortunately, the past two decades have also given rise to several new forces that our society can build on to strengthen sound public judgment. Three new developments are particularly noteworthy.

A New Social Movement
The first development is the growth of a concerted effort to advance what its leading participants call "deliberative democracy." The core principles of deliberative democracy are the same as those advanced in *Coming to Public Judgment*: faith in democracy and in the potential wisdom of the public voice; a conviction that the dominant, simple-minded model of how public opinion is formed is depriving the citizenry of the opportunity to make up their minds in a thoughtful fashion; a desire to develop a more realistic model of the public learning curve; and an eagerness to develop new methods to enhance the quality of public opinion by giving the public more opportunities to deliberate thoughtfully.

There is, however, one important difference of emphasis between the theories advanced in *Coming to Public Judgment* and those of the deliberative democracy movement. It concerns the meaning and widespread use of the term "deliberative." This term conjures up a picture of people engaged in a highly dispassionate cognitive process, where irrationality and emotions have been effectively set aside. My own experience runs counter to this image. Hundreds of studies of public opinion have convinced me that the public's learning curve is not a dispassionately rational process. Instead, it is charged with all manner of emotion and irrationality. This is sometimes negative—people must wrestle with wishful thinking, denial, pride, stubbornness, and cognitive dissonance. But it is also positive—bringing passion, energy, sympathy, and enthusiasm into the picture.

So I wince a bit at the word "deliberative." But this difference of emphasis is just a nuance. Overall, I believe that the deliberative democracy movement is making a vitally important contribution to the nation's thinking about how to achieve sound public judgment.

Better Research Methods

A second positive development is closely linked to the first. Since the 1991 book came out, the practitioners represented in the essays in the current book have been busy developing new techniques for assessing public opinion that take the complexities of the learning curve into full account. We need new methods of accelerating public opinion formation—new ways of helping the public advance along the learning curve in the interest of solving our nation's problems in a timely fashion.

The chapters that follow describe some promising and fascinating new techniques. They include a variety of methods for helping cross sections of the public work their way through all stages of the learning curve.

Improved Theoretical Underpinnings

Another promising development in recent years comes from the domain of theory. In recent years, thinkers from a variety of disciplines have challenged one of Western culture's most deeply embedded assumptions: the sharp dichotomy between thought and emotion.

It is impossible to exaggerate how influential this distinction has been in shaping the core ideas of European and American civilization, and how deep its roots are. They trace back to Plato more than 2,500 years ago. In Plato's classic Myth of the Cave, the inhabitants of the cave mistake the shadows on its walls for reality. It is their senses and emotions that lead them to that erroneous conclusion, in contrast to the rational mind's gift for understanding that the reality outside the shadows of the cave is vastly different. Throughout the centuries, this myth has been reworked in countless ways, but always with the persistent split between mind and body, reason and emotion, logic and passionate conviction, fact and value.

This sharp distinction between the cognitive and emotional domains relies on a deeply flawed epistemological assumption. According to this view (which has dominated the social sciences for decades), the cognitive side is equated with science, reason, and ideas stripped of emotion. The emotive side is seen as "nonrational" and is generally devalued. The result is a widespread assumption that emotions are out of place in reaching sound decisions.

It is only in recent years that a variety of disciplines, such as philosophy, cognitive psychology, and neuroscience, have challenged the validity of this widespread distinction. Martha Nussbaum, the philosopher, has flatly stated that the distinction is unwarranted.[2] Philosopher Hilary Putnam has called into question the fact/value distinction that lies at the heart of traditional social science.[3] Daniel Goleman's book *Emotional Intelligence* sums up the work of a number of cognitive psychologists on the role that emotion plays in shaping people's understanding of life and other people.[4] Most compellingly, the work of Antonio Damasio and other neuroscientists has demonstrated that emotions are essential to sound decision making.[5] Not only are emotions not a hindrance to judgment, but sophisticated brain research shows that you can't reach sound judgment without them.

Emotion is therefore not something that gets in the way of sound judgment: it is indispensable to it. Judgments that do not draw on the emotional centers of the brain tend to be deeply flawed. For decades we have gotten the fact/value distinction all wrong.

Our work in the field of public opinion provides powerful reinforcement of these scientific discoveries and analyses. As I have already noted, there is much more to sound public judgment than factually informed public opinion. People arrive at sound judgment only when they have aligned their views on important issues with their core values—an emotion-laden process. However well informed they may be from a factual point of view, if they haven't carried out this emotional task, they have not reached sound public judgment. For example, while most Americans have accepted the fact that human activity contributes to global warming, they have not yet completed the difficult emotional work needed to act on this knowledge.

Unfortunately, while our society is well equipped to carry out the task of conveying information, it is not well equipped to help the public carry out its emotion-laden working-through process. Partly this is because our culture doesn't even recognize the need to do so. Conveying information to the public and helping it work though the emotional side of decision making necessitates very different institutions, methods, and time requirements. The essays that follow illuminate how public engagement can be carried out more effectively and how citizens can be helped to achieve sound public judgment.

Priorities

The stakes could hardly be higher. If the United States is to maintain a leadership role in the world, it must master the problems that now threaten to overwhelm us. Most of these are time-gap problems—energy, global warming, an enormous and growing debt, health care and education reform, immigration, financial regulation, our conflict with the Muslim world, and so on.

The role of the public is critical to the successful resolution of all these issues. Potentially, the public can contribute in ways that elude expert elites and leaders. The public brings to the table a down-to-earth practicality, a nonideological pragmatic focus, and a strong insistence on the values that hold our society together. With sound public judgment, the public voice is a tremendous force for good, a reaffirmation of a healthy and vital democracy. Without sound public judgment, the public voice becomes part of the problem rather than part of the solution.

I've asked myself a simple, realistic question: If those responsible for shaping public opinion—political leadership, the media, scientists, civic and business leaders, other experts—could only do one thing to advance the quality of public judgment in the United States, what would that one thing be?

The one requirement for exercising public judgment that the public needs most (and utterly lacks) is a limited number of credible choices for working through each of the emotion-laden time-gap issues cited earlier. "Limited" means not more than three or four choices. I have come to think of these as *value choices*, as distinct from policy options of the sort familiar to technical experts, because the value aspect of each choice is central.

Those of us who have been long-term students of the public mind are aware of the gaping disconnect between the kind of information that rains down on the public every day and the kinds of choices people need to make up their minds and arrive at sound judgment on complex issues. Let me illustrate with two time-gap issues—energy and our relations with the Muslim world.

Energy

In the coming decades, the American public will confront one fateful decision after another in coping with the energy challenge. On the personal level, people are likely to continue to shift out of SUVs to smaller, more fuel-efficient vehicles, and when convenient to opt for public transportation instead of driving. At the policy level, they will be weighing in on decisions with regard to greater national energy independence so as to slow the transfer of hundreds of billions of dollars a year to nations hostile to our interests. They will also be weighing the pros and cons of greater reliance on nuclear energy and other alternative fuels that may be controversial and costly and could require subsidies. They will be considering the pros and cons of offshore drilling (especially in light of the recent oil disaster in the Gulf of Mexico), ethanol, biofuels, coal, the development of electric cars, greater reliance on wind farms, substituting natural gas for coal in generating electricity, and so forth. All these decisions are value laden. Most require some degree of sacrifice and change of behavior. They are not easy decisions, especially with special interests muddying the waters.

This is a subject that is receiving enormous amounts of attention and media coverage. The media are performing their consciousness-raising task with vigor and effectiveness. But no one is giving the public the kinds of overarching choices that people need to arrive at sensible, pragmatic judgments.

Clearly, one choice is to give priority to the national security aspects of the problem and radically reduce our reliance on imported oil. This choice would involve far greater dependence on both conservation and developing the energy resources available to us domestically, including coal, natural gas, oil, nuclear power, and alternative energy sources such as wind and solar power.

A second choice would be to give priority to global climate change. This would involve less dependence on heavy-polluting coal and more on our abundant sources of less polluting natural gas as a transition fuel for the next ten to fifteen years while we aggressively develop alternative energy sources (including nuclear power).

A third choice is to put economic growth ahead of these other threats and try to muddle through with more conservation, greater energy efficiency, and development of alternative sources of energy, without doing much to reduce our dependence on imported oil.

There are countless ways to tweak these choices and to balance their competing demands, but our core values will ultimately determine our judgment. Some Americans will give priority to the national security threat posed by our transferring so much of our wealth to oil-producing nations hostile to our interests. Others will want to give priority to the daunting threat that global climate change poses. Others have as their primary consideration keeping the costs of our energy consumption as low as possible. The nation's political and civic leaders have an obligation to get the public to focus on these mind-boggling alternatives and come to judgment on how best to balance them, because nothing less than our future well-being may be at stake.

Relations with the Muslim World

Equally fateful choices confront us on how to manage our troubled relations with the Muslim world. Our use of military force in three Muslim countries and our threats against yet another (Iran) give credibility to the claims of Muslim extremists that the United States is at war with Islam, has no respect for Muslim values and beliefs, and is trying to impose our alien culture on the Muslim world. These claims inflame Muslim public opinion and undermine the efforts of moderate clerics and political leaders to rein in extremism. Muslim extremists have successfully made us scapegoats for the failure of so many Muslim nations to build their own just and prosperous societies.

Without this broader support, the extremists represent fewer than 10 percent of the world's 1.4 billion Muslims. Gallup public opinion data show that the great majority of Muslims disapprove of attacks on civilians and venerate the Abrahamic faith they share with the Judeo-Christian tradition as a guide to righteousness and morality.

There is widespread agreement in the United States that a successful strategy for isolating extremists cannot rely exclusively on military force. When our forces in Muslim countries help to build wells and schools and then bomb insurgents, accidentally killing civilians, our intentions are certain to be mistrusted. Over the past few years, more and more Americans (now up to 65 percent) have come to believe that we have placed too much emphasis on military force and not enough on political, diplomatic, and economic initiatives.

Here, too, the public should be given an opportunity to wrestle with three choices—a military/diplomatic approach, another based on economic modernization, and a containment option that combines elements of the other two.

The military/diplomatic choice is based on the assumption that extremists such as Al Qaeda and elements of the Taliban are irreconcilable foes and can be defeated only through military means. While we cannot rely *exclusively* on our military strategy, nothing else will work if we don't have a successful military engagement against the insurgency. We should, of course, follow up with vigorous diplomacy designed to stabilize Muslim nations torn apart by extremism.

The economic modernization choice favors a strategy that emphasizes helping Islamic nations modernize and build prosperous societies. Proponents of this choice believe that if we could somehow extricate ourselves from an active military role in Muslim nations, build bridges of understanding to peaceful Islamists (like those currently in power in Turkey), provide assistance to Muslim communities, as we did to great effect after the tsunami devastated coastal areas of Indonesia, and above all help modernize Muslim economies, the extremists would find themselves increasingly isolated.

Many Muslim nations harbor a growing middle class with ambitious economic aspirations. They are much more interested in encouraging economic development, trade, and investment than in waging ideological war against the United States. We should be able to demonstrate to these nations that they have much to gain economically from constructive relations with the United States.

The third choice would adapt the containment-type strategy that worked so well against the Soviet Union. Proponents of this choice believe that a political policy of containment implemented with the aid of strong, like-minded allies can eventually succeed in our struggle against Muslim extremism. The West managed to win the Cold War by standing firm and setting an example of the benefits of free society that eventually overcame ideological fanaticism. That is what we must now do to defeat terrorism, prevent states ruled by unstable dictators from acquiring and spreading the means of mass destruction, and restore our standing as the world's leading democracy.

In implementing this largely political strategy, we must not make the mistake of assuming that Muslim equals Arab. Arab nations make up only a fraction of the Muslim world. Our chances of forming much more positive relations with non-Arab Muslims, such as those in Indonesia and Turkey (and possibly even Iran), may be far better than with Arab nations. Taking advantage of the Arab/non-Arab divide in the Muslim world can help to advance a political containment policy.

In summary, practitioners of public opinion research like me have learned that nothing advances the public's learning curve more effectively than the opportunity to discuss and deliberate a specific set of choices, with their value implications cogently set forth.

We have policy think tanks galore that set forth technical options for leadership. We have precious few that formulate *value choices for the public.* But fortunately, those we do have are well represented in the chapters that follow.

CHAPTER 2

Further Reflections

A Dialogue between Dan Yankelovich and Will Friedman

Will: It's probably impossible to trace in any comprehensive way, but how did your perspective on public opinion, public judgment, and democratic process come about?

Dan: My interest started in graduate school. Several of my professors at Harvard had developed an interest in how people form opinions, particularly the deeper psychological roots of their opinions. I became interested in the conflicts between people's basic values deriving from their life experiences versus their opinions that reflected the views popular in the media.

In 1949, I decided to take a leave of absence from Harvard and attend the Sorbonne in Paris. To save money for my Paris sojourn, I got a job as a junior member of a team of psychologists hired by MIT to find out why so many returning vets were dropping out of MIT or having difficulty adapting to student life. I enjoyed interviewing the MIT students (veterans like me) and identifying the sources of their adjustment problems. And I was impressed by the diligence, care, and speed with which the MIT administration implemented our findings. This planted the seeds for the kind of work I would do in the future.

When I moved to New York in 1952 I worked at an industrial design firm. The head of the firm had developed a concept he called "pre-design research," which was to find out through interviewing what kinds of features people wanted in the products the firm designed. In the course of doing that sort of interviewing, we were often asked to estimate the potential market for new products. If you simply asked consumers, "Would you buy X?" and acted on their answers, it would be (and often was) a disastrous mistake for the companies making the products. So I learned to use poll questions as the *starting point*, not the end point, for understanding the link between consumer intentions and their actual behavior.

I applied that lesson to the political field in the 1960 election, when I conducted an experiment based on my experience that polls estimating the market for new products can be misleading. The polls at the time showed Jack Kennedy behind Richard Nixon by four points. I recruited and interviewed a random sample of four hundred voters in Syracuse. I asked each one the traditional polling question, "If the election were held tomorrow, who would you vote for, the Republican candidate, Richard Nixon, or the democratic candidate, Jack Kennedy?" Then I started a discussion with them. I brought up the themes that were in the air and were working their way into the campaign. I said, "This is early in the campaign. Let's discuss some of the problems that people are concerned about, such as Jack Kennedy's Catholicism, his lack of experience in foreign policy, Richard Nixon's style, and the references to him as Tricky Dick." The purpose of the discussion was to give each voter a chance to "work through" conflicting feelings. At the end of the discussion, which typically took about an hour with each respondent, I said, "All right, now that you've had a chance to think about it, whom do you think you might vote for?"

Most of the Syracuse voters didn't change their minds, but some did. The results came out fifty-fifty, which is really the way the election turned out. That was in 1960. So I started to think about the "working-through" process in the 1950s and early 1960s, which eventually made its way into the *Public Judgment* book many years later.

Will: So the first known experiment combining deliberation and polling happened in 1960! Had you written any articles, anything prior to the *Public Judgment* book that dealt with the concept of "working through," or was this happening more in your consciousness but not being articulated?

Dan: In 1960 I also wrote a piece for *Life* magazine on the ideal president, and that also dealt with the working-through phenomenon. The piece I wrote for the *Harvard Business Review* in 1964 on new nondemographic methods of segmentation was not directly focused on working through, but there was some development of it. I would say that the beginning of these ideas for me was my market and political research experience in the 1950s.

I wrote my *Public Judgment* book before Jim Fishkin developed his deliberative democracy polls. When I discussed it with him, he said he was sorry he hadn't read the book, because if he had, he would have credited it with anticipating what he was trying to do. Not being credited didn't bother me. It illustrates the process that when something is in the air, it is going to gestate in many minds.

It's sobering, though, to see how long it took. Let's say that scientific public opinion polling began pretty much in the 1930s. It caught the nation's attention after the 1936 election, when a Gallup survey of a few thousand voters correctly predicted a Roosevelt victory. The *Literary Digest* had conducted a poll with a vastly larger sample of voters. But they polled only voters who owned telephones—a luxury in the 1930s. It predicted a landslide for Alfred Landon. The *Literary Digest* never recovered from that fiasco and went out of business. That was the dramatic entry of scientific public opinion polling into our political life.

Will: When did you actually get into the field?

Dan: I entered the field in the early 1950s. The pioneers in the field were Gallup, Roper, Crossley, Hadley Cantril, and others who began their work in the 1930s. Gallup became interested in the quality of public opinion early on, but then dropped the subject. The pressures of the field were such that he abandoned his initial interest. When I picked up the topic in *Coming to Public Judgment*, it received a dismissive one-paragraph review in the *Journal of the American Association of Public Opinion Research* (AAPOR) whose theme was "Why is Yankelovich being so perverse?"

At the time, the public opinion profession was busy with technical issues involved with measuring, sampling, question wording, question sequence, bias, etc. My concern about the quality of public opinion seemed to come out of left field. The dominant attitude was, "Why do we have to deal with this? We have more urgent matters to contend with." I acknowledged the importance of technical issues, but they were really minor compared with how you make democracy work, how you make public opinion sounder and more thoughtful. In contrast to practitioners in the public opinion field, the journalist and philosopher Walter Lippmann had anticipated my concern. He influenced me, and I began "worrying" the issue.

Will: Were you worrying it before you began to practice public opinion research or as a *result* of practice? To what extent did you bring it with you, and to what extent did it emerge out of what you were seeing?

Dan: I brought a lot of it with me. My background was different from the background of most people in the polling profession. I was trained in psychology and philosophy, not statistics. From a psychological point of view, the notion that people are working through issues, struggling with them, dealing with the rational and irrational at the same time came directly from studies in personality development. My background and training in philosophy gave me a concern for the nature of opinion as knowledge, the epistemological side of the issue.

Will: Let me ask you something about your psychology background and the working-through metaphor. My recollection is that you originally were using the working-through metaphor in a psychoanalytic sense, of people working through internal resistances toward liberating insight.

Dan: That is correct. That's where the concept comes from. I sometimes use the following example: A wife leaves a note on the refrigerator door saying, "I'm leaving your dinner in the fridge." The husband returns, sees the note, and absorbs the information immediately in real time. But suppose the wife leaves an even shorter note on the refrigerator door that simply says, "I'm leaving you." The husband reads the note, but it may take him months or years to fully absorb it.

Will: Actually, that example is relevant to why I brought it up, because the process of working through is not all about loss and coming to terms with it. There certainly is some of that—the loss of easy answers, the need to accept trade-offs and sacrifices. But there is also a sense of building something new—common ground, creative breakthroughs, new ways of working together and moving forward—that does not map quite as well to working through in the sense of loss and grief. There's a lot that's fun and liberating about working through as well as a lot that's hard and harrowing.

Dan: I think that's right. Of course, all metaphors are imperfect. Psychoanalytic theory and personality development theory basically revolve around struggling with difficult emotional issues, so the "work" idea in the phrase "working through" appealed to me. That part of it I brought with me as I entered the field of public opinion.

Will: You can see how one idea led to the other. And how did you then come to decide to embody these kinds of ideas in an organization?

Dan: I was friends with Cyrus Vance when he headed up his New York law firm. We met regularly for lunch. At one of our luncheons in 1975, he and I talked about the deplorable fact that the main issue in the upcoming presidential campaign focused on two tiny islands in the Formosa Straits, Quemoy and Matsu. All other issues were being pushed to the side.

So we discussed what we thought were the most important issues for the campaign. We felt that the issues that needed more voter attention were the economy (inflation and unemployment), the general direction of our foreign policy, and an issue that we called "moral leadership in government." It was at this lunch that we talked about what a good thing it would be to be able to get a better understanding of how the public felt about these issues and share that information with the candidates. And that's what we did. We launched an ad hoc entity that we tentatively called the Public Agenda Foundation.[1] Public Agenda's first product was three briefing books analyzing public opinion on these topics.

We were very encouraged by the fact that both major candidates, Gerald Ford and Jimmy Carter, used the briefing books in their presidential debates. President Carter made Vance his secretary of state, which was in part a result of this work. The briefing books were not the only reason, but they were an important reason. Public Agenda began to take shape as an organization from then on.

Will: This brings us to one of the designs of this book, which is to look at several organizations that have explicitly used the ideas you developed as a point of departure for applied work. Looking at these three organizational applications—Public Agenda, the National Issues Forums, and Viewpoint Learning—what strikes you?

Dan: I am interested in the fact that the three organizations each took somewhat different tacks. For instance, the three have placed different emphases on whether to work directly with the public or to concentrate primarily on leadership, and they affect the public indirectly as a result. All of these efforts attempt to fill a gap in our society. To me, it's a bit startling that we have so many societal institutions devoted to consciousness raising [Stage I of the public judgment model] and almost a total absence of institutions devoted to the working-through aspect [Stage II].

I see all of our efforts as representing different kinds of probes. There's a lot of room for a variety of probes, and particularly for research to assess their relative effectiveness. For example, the aspect that you've been personally dedicated to—the engagement part of it—is at the pioneering stage of finding new ways to mobilize public engagement. I wish that academic political science would devote more attention to the institution-building aspect of public judgment, but you are illuminating an important aspect of it.

What we don't know is how far you can go. One of the things that help people come to judgment is clarifying the choices that the country needs to be making. Preparing choices for public deliberation involves a tremendous amount of work. We sometimes minimize its importance because it's only a tool, but actually it should not be minimized because it's essential. One of the reasons that "working through" can stretch out over years is the relative absence of the right choices, with their pros and cons clearly laid out for people.

Will: What makes for a right version as opposed to a not-helpful version of that? What are the criteria?

Dan: The news coverage of how to deal with the banking crisis is a prime example of how *not* to present choices that the public can wrestle with. From the public's point of view, the right choices define the issues from the perspective of *values* rather than from a technical perspective. Choosing among various forms of capitalizing the banks is too technical for the public. The choices for the public would have to be in terms of what values are served. For example, should we really be rewarding the very people who are responsible for the banks' failures? The moral hazard issue is important to people.

Will: You're using the language "What's important to people." There's a bit of an art, as well as maybe the beginning of a science, in how to frame choices. A number of us do it and work on it—and I think we have an intuitive sense of what we're doing—but I don't think the methodology is that well articulated yet.

Dan: What we're doing is starting from the public's point of departure. If you start from the bankers' point of view, you get a different set of choices. Whether you do it formally or informally, by hunch or through a formal research process, you're trying to do the same thing: you're taking the public's starting point and framing choices from its perspective.

Another consideration is that you can't have a lot of choices—for example, five or six choices would be too many.

Also essential is that the values involved be an important—and explicit—basis for the choices. Because that is what citizens are best qualified to judge. You could easily write a PhD thesis on the whole matter of citizen choices versus technical policy options—where they differ, where they're similar, and where there's some overlap. What's troubling me about the current economic crisis is the opaqueness of choices *either* from a public *or* from a policy point of view. The science of economics is not nearly as advanced as most economists like to believe. There isn't a good enough understanding of the way the economy really works.

Will: This example of the economic crisis poses a challenge for the outcome-oriented perspective you bring to the process of engaging the public. An essential aspect of the argument and theory is that people need to come to terms with the consequences of their choices. It's always possible to point out some of them, but often with issues on the cusp of science or economics, we simply don't know all the consequences of going down one road versus another.

Dan: Of course, there are some consequences that are fairly clear to experts. As a citizen I delegate to the experts the task of bringing thought, time, and attention to this question as well as technical knowledge.

Will: The question remains, though, how to help the public come to terms with issues where we need to make decisions and take action even when the consequences are not known with great certainty. From the standpoint of helping citizens come to judgment, we know it's important to help people understand the reasonably well-known consequences. But how important is it to communicate and be up front about the fact that there are liable to be unexpected, unintended things that we'll have to deal with as well, so that people don't feel betrayed when the unexpected pops up?

Dan: I think people live with uncertainty every day. That's part of life, so I would say yes, we can address the fact that there are consequences of different policies and we know something about them, but there's also lots of uncertainty.

Suppose you were to say, "Look, we feel that the Keynesian perspective is very well founded. We have confidence that however we spend the money, it is going to make a difference, it's going to accomplish one of our objectives, which is to turn the economy around. But there's also another objective, which is to use the money prudently and wisely for the future—that's different." I don't see why we can't make the uncertainty explicit.

Will: Of course, it goes directly against the grain of political rhetoric to admit that there's less than perfect certainty.

Dan: But you're trying to do something different from governance-as-usual. People can deal with that.

Will: Agreed. I want to go back to an early statement you made about how little capacity we have as a society for helping the public "work through" issues. What are your hypotheses about why that is? Is it strictly a lack of understanding? Is it lack of incentive? Are some people advantaged by the public not working through?

Dan: Our existing institutions reflect the dominant theory of the media that *information* is the key to public judgment. Their belief is that helping people reach sound judgment is a reasonably simple transaction. You give them information and they make up their minds. According to this theory, it's the job of journalists to make issues clear, but once they are clear, there's no reason why people—if they pay attention—shouldn't get it. Since there's no room for "working through" in this theory, there is no need for institutions to help people do it.

The theory is incredibly wrong, and yet it seems to persist forever. For the last three or four decades, I haven't been able to get over the fact that it's so wrong and that there's so little willingness to look at it. Why should such an erroneous theory persist against all evidence? The people in the information business have a stake in the importance of information. And journalists always like to quote the Jeffersonian dictum that a well-informed citizenry is indispensable to democracy.

Will: Although you feel that's often a misinterpreted phrase.

Dan: That's right. Jefferson meant something different, something much richer and thicker. For Jefferson, being well informed meant thought and good judgment as well as information. But that's the sort of nuance that tends to go by the boards. Journalists look at you like you're crazy when you say that information is not the key to reaching sound judgment.

Will: Let me try to add another layer to this discussion: the question of power and how it intersects with what you're saying. I agree with your analysis that the culture of expertise accounts for a great deal of why the public's voice has been minimized in the democratic process. But I also tend to feel that other factors need to be woven in if we're to have a complete picture, not only theoretically, but in terms of practice and trying to have impact with this work. It seems to me that exacerbating or interplaying with the culture-of-expertise problem are various kinds of power issues and dynamics. Interest group politics is part of this, as are deeper "structural" cultural assumptions that advantage some folks and disadvantage others.

For instance, there is the intentional manipulation of the public from interest group and partisan politics, with everybody spinning the facts to their advantage, that constrains the public's and society's ability to come to judgment. Thus, for example, the unwillingness of the cigarette companies to admit for so many years that smoking poses a health hazard was not due to the fact that they didn't understand how to bring it to the public. The problem wasn't that they thought information was the key to public judgment, it was that misinformation was key to their interests. It seems to me that if the power factor is not woven into our theory more explicitly, we will be less effective than we want to be. There's a way in which the work of helping the public come to judgment is partly about breaking out of the lock of power on public thinking.

Dan: The extreme use of power is the denial of democracy, so I absolutely agree about the importance of power. You'd have to be naive not to agree, but our society understands power politics better than it does the importance of deliberation and working through in arriving at sound public judgment

Will: At Public Agenda, as you know, we're playing with the distinction between "public consultation" modes of deliberation work and "public engagement modes."[2] One of the reasons we're wrestling with this distinction comes from a frustration with the reality of power as it intersects with public judgment formation. As we or others work to engage citizens and help them work through issues, we are then in the position of having to sit back and wait and see if leaders respond to it, beyond perfunctory acknowledgments about how wonderful it is to see citizens engaged. And they may be impressed with what they see citizens doing, but they're also so locked into the typical ways in which decisions get made that citizen deliberation may not, in the end, have much real impact on decisions. Our thinking is that there are actually *multiple* actors who can learn from and "leverage" citizen engagement for constructive action, such as civil society organizations and "grass tips" leaders and citizens themselves, not just traditional, official decision makers. And as more and different kinds of people become active as a result of this kind of work, more momentum can build, and we can find ways to have an impact despite the tendency for typical power dynamics to short-circuit forward progress.

Dan: The strength of direct public engagement is that you're actually moving the public itself toward a more thoughtful position. The limitation is that everybody can get frustrated, because the public is only willing to make that effort if they feel it's going to mean something and if other conditions are right, and that can be a slow and arduous process. The advantage of working directly with policy makers is that you don't have an extra step. You are engaging the leaders from the get-go, but it may not be the ideal way of engaging the public. I agree that it's an important distinction. The ideal would be to do both: to brief leaders about the public's deepest concerns and also to actually engage the public as a way of tackling the working-through process.

That said, in the long run, if what you're trying to do is strengthen the democratic process so that it functions better, then you do have to focus on strengthening the public side. To me, if you can strengthen the public side and improve the quality of public judgment, that's a win-win for everybody. Descriptively, power is omnipresent. Prescriptively, what you want to do is to give more influence and credibility to the public voice, and what you are doing through these processes of public engagement is precisely that.

It occurs to me that heeding the public voice has a different significance for various levels of leadership. Take, for example, health care and the interests of the Obama administration and those of experts and leaders in the health care field. The closer you come to the pragmatic criterion of what works, the more feasible it is to bring the public and the leadership together. Practically, on this point, I think you can see a big difference between members of Congress and the governors of states.

Will: You are suggesting that governors can be more pragmatic and people in Congress can be more ideological—that kind of idea?

Dan: Yes, Congress can be more ideological, more interested in power plays, less driven by results. Achieving pragmatic results is the friend of public engagement. The leaders who have a stake in actually getting things done are going to be more responsive than the leaders who have other interests. We should resist making the criterion of success one of electability or bipartisanship or some other structural consideration. We need to focus on results.

In the waning days of the Bush administration, the low ratings in the polls for Bush really undermined his effective leadership. It deprived him of the bully pulpit that's so important a part of the presidency. Every time you talk about power and influence, my mind keeps coming back to the criterion of what works, what gets results.

Will: That seems very useful as a way to think about the work strategically and also as a compelling way to communicate about it.

Dan: It does seem helpful, because one of the compelling features of the public voice, from a democracy point of view, is its practicality and pragmatism. Americans have a "Chinese menu" approach to issues: one from column A (liberal), one from column B (conservative). People are more concerned about results than they are about ideology and power dynamics and all that other stuff. From that perspective, you can get an alignment of interest between the public and those leaders who are also focused on results.

There's a great deal more work to be done on what you call the consultative aspect of the connection to leadership. We have learned a lot. We have the technical means to be able to tell leaders what choices the public will make when it reaches judgment.

In a way, the two strands [of informing leaders and engaging the public] begin to merge. The leadership has its own working-through process, so it isn't like you can just send them a report through the mail. Let's say, for example, you have a president who's not an economist himself but who has a lot of economic advisers. All his economic advisers are telling him that the most efficient way to cut gasoline use is to raise the price. Technically, I'm sure they're right. I'm also sure that it would mean political suicide. The reaction of the public would be, "You must be insane!" The problem for the public is that gas costs too much. Our way of life is suburban. We've built our lifestyle around the availability of reasonably priced gas. Okay, maybe we have to put up with some countries like Saudi Arabia gouging us. But for our own government to add to the price of gas is simply unthinkable from the public's perspective.

Will: Leaders have to see it.

Dan: They have to see it. They have to work it through. They have to absorb it and then they have to say, "You say that the public will accept positive incentives, but they don't accept what they would regard as punitive measures. Would such and such work as an incentive?" You might say, "No, it wouldn't, because it's a hidden form of punishment." So there's a back-and-forth to help the leader think through how to act on what you're telling him or her.

You might say, "Mr. President, I think what you're proposing would be acceptable if it isn't too big a bite for any one time. If you're asking people to change and make sacrifices, they may recognize the need in theory. They might go along with it if you do it slowly, in baby steps." It puts you in a position of not only reporting data, but also understanding how to get to the goal. Part of the deliberative democracy mission is how to help leaders lead democratically to reach the objectives that best serve the country.

Will: Just as an exercise, how would the conversation you're describing differ from the conversation the president would have with his trusted political public opinion adviser about a policy issue? I think they're likely to be close cousins, but there are some distinctions as well.

Dan: Eventually the public opinion advisers will be people like you, whose task is to work with leaders to help them understand deeper dimensions of public judgment than conventional polls allow. That's where the field will move.

Will: A few moments ago you spoke about the types of leaders who are likely to be amenable to the kind of work we do because they are more results oriented and less ideologically driven. Do you think there are ways to expand the pool of such leaders, to change the incentives and culture among leadership to tilt it more toward the pragmatic perspective?

Dan: It's useful to limit our ambitions. If the factor that aligns the public interest with leadership is their common interest in results, then the task is to find leaders who see it as their responsibility to achieve real results. If, for example, you can align the governors and the president and other national leaders together, you've accomplished more than anybody could reasonably expect you to accomplish. You don't have to align everybody.

Will: Fair enough. In your chapter in this book you note that there are a lot more people working on these problems than there used to be. There's a whole field or movement, the deliberative democracy movement. I'd like to hear a little more about what heartens you about the deliberative democracy field, what worries you about it, and what advice would you offer the field.

Dan: I do have this somewhat quirky resistance to the word "deliberative," because it conjures up an image that's too rational, too deliberative, too thoughtful, too balanced, too reflective. That's been the problem with economic theory and its image of the rational economic actor, which has led it down the garden path over and over again. People's minds are much more stormy and emotional. Part of our contribution is to describe the process as it really exists, because it's credible once you can describe the way people act in real life.

Will: On that question, one of the things I've noticed in looking at the field is that the practitioners are essentially with you. The different organizations that are actually doing the work in communities understand that it's not a purely rational process. Some of this is a split between some academic theorists and the practitioners, and they need to become a little more fully integrated. This is slowly beginning to happen as more conferences and associations bring practitioners and academics together.[3]

Dan: That's good. Often the academics are somewhat behind, which goes against the stereotype.

In looking at the deliberative democracy movement I would also hope that the different actors don't fall too much in love with their particular methods and techniques. Whatever their devices are, they're all just techniques. The larger point is to describe the process and the principles accurately and develop a variety of techniques that can be used in a variety of circumstances.

I also would not want to denigrate the common, garden-variety public opinion poll too much because it is extremely cost effective. If you want to understand the views of the country, the most economical way to do so is through the well-established approach to polling. The standards and procedures are set. The one change I would make would be to try to find a practical way to get across the idea that poll results can be misleading if people have yet to make up their minds. You cannot tell now from looking at most polls whether people have or have not made up their mind about an issue. There are various techniques that are not complicated for giving that indication, and I think using them would address a major weakness of polling.

Will: Obviously we agree at Public Agenda that polls can be useful, and we're still using surveys. In doing so we try to be mindful of your point that it's critical to know whether or not people have thought much about an issue they are being asked about.

At the same time, we also increasingly see polling as a step in service to larger purposes of public or stakeholder engagement. For more and more projects, we're thinking of it as a kind of "starting-point" research, the beginning of a process that not only informs policy debates with respect to where the public is right now, but also informs efforts to engage citizens to help them come to deeper terms with issues. In your language, focus groups and polls can be both a way to determine where people are on the "learning curve" of an issue and a guide to how to help them move along it.

Which brings us to the "learning curve" concept and language. There are ways in which I like and ways in which I'm a bit wary of the learning curve terminology. It's a strong way to counteract the weakness in traditional polling you were just speaking of, the tendency to forget that the public has to go through a process to come to terms with an issue, and we need to understand where the public is in that process if we're to meaningfully understand the results of a poll. The one thing I worry about, though, is the danger of journalists and others taking "learning" in a very flat sense that puts them in the same culture-of-expertise mind-set that you wrote *Coming to Public Judgment* in part to counteract: that the public simply needs more information, that most people are deficient experts and simply need more facts and figures to see the light.

Dan: It's a good point. You're asking if I'm falling into a trap with the concept of the learning curve because it may imply a strongly rationalistic, information-based process. It need not do so as long as you're explicit about the nature of the learning that needs to take place. The notion of learning from experience is very well established and people understand it. So we need to associate the learning curve idea with that. You can say that the learning process is a stormy one and it's more closely associated with learning from life experience than it is with absorbing information.

Will: Another way in which the entire public judgment construct can be misunderstood, I believe, is that it can connote a monolithic view of the public, which raises a number of questions. Where is minority opinion within the public judgment framework? Are we in danger of rolling over people's differences if we focus on the "public's" judgment in some broad sense? When is it useful to talk about *the* public versus *many* publics?

Dan: It's a very important point. One of the things I tried to do in my book on dialogue was to insist that the purpose of dialogue is not consensus.[4] It's not that everybody's going to think the same way at the end of even the best of dialogues. It's that at the end of the dialogue process, they may end up with even sharper disagreement than when they started, but they also end up with a better understanding of differing viewpoints.

One of the empirical things that impressed me, and I would not have predicted, is that dialogue almost always leads to more respect for the differing points of view. The process of coming to judgment through dialogue rather than advocacy creates a climate of civility. It creates civic virtue. So it becomes one of those issues you have to clarify: we're not looking for consensus but for better understanding of differing perspectives, for taking others' views into account. This is one of the reasons I have such great respect for Barack Obama, because I believe he personifies that ability.

Will: Any final thoughts you'd like to share?

Dan: I'd like to emphasize the point I made in my chapter, namely, that our society is faced with an unprecedented number of what I call "time-gap issues" such as energy, global warming, an enormous and growing debt, health care and education reform, immigration, financial regulation, our conflict with the Muslim world, etc. These time-gap issues have an urgency that outstrips the time the public ordinarily requires to reach sound judgment on them. We desperately need innovations to accelerate the public's learning curve so as to give citizens the opportunity to reach sound judgment on complex problems in a timely fashion. I believe that experimentation in achieving this goal is the most important underlying theme of this book.

PART II

APPLICATIONS

CHAPTER 3

The Experience of the National Issues Forums

KEITH MELVILLE AND ROBERT J. KINGSTON

It is not often that the framework and assertions made in any book are tested repeatedly over a period of twenty-eight years, in hundreds of different settings. Yet that is what has happened in the case of Dan Yankelovich's seminal book of 1991, *Coming to Public Judgment*. In many ways, the ideas in his book—its critique of the limitations of public opinion, its instructions about public deliberation, and the argument it makes about why deliberation is a key element in moving to public judgment about critical issues—were formative influences in shaping the National Issues Forums (NIF), a popular nationwide network that began in the early 1980s and continues to this day.

Although *Coming to Public Judgment* was not published until 1991, it was a work in progress throughout the 1980s. In 1981, Dan Yankelovich and his colleagues at Public Agenda began working with David Mathews, who had just become president of the Kettering Foundation. Under his leadership, in collaboration with representatives of seventeen community-based organizations that had first met in the summer of 1981 at the Wingspread Conference Center in Wisconsin, what would later become the National Issues Forums was started. This nonpartisan consortium, which in its early years was called the Domestic Policy Association, had convened to form a nationwide network of forums that would focus public discussion each year on a number of pressing national issues.

During NIF's first two decades, Public Agenda helped select the issues and prepared brief, balanced, and accessible magazine-style issue books, a task now undertaken each year by a variety of staff and consultants associated with the Kettering Foundation. Each issue book presents three or four distinctive "choices" or approaches to a controversial public issue, providing a framework for public discussion and a catalyst for deliberation. They are meant as a vehicle for moving people toward public judgment.

The NIF network, which began as a partnership involving a handful of communities, has grown substantially over the years. No longer a start-up enterprise, NIF and the public forums that convene under its auspices are a familiar and well-established part of hundreds of communities across the United States. Since their inception, National Issues Forums have addressed more than eighty issues and have taken place in almost every state.[1] NIF, which was one of the few groups to embrace public deliberation in the early 1980s, continues to have a prominent role in what has become a multifaceted effort, now sometimes characterized as the civic renewal or deliberative democracy movement. The groups in this movement, starting with NIF and now including dozens of other deliberative efforts, have created forms of civic practice that are, according to sociologists Carmen Sirianni and Lewis Friedland, "far more sophisticated in grappling with complex public problems and collaborating with diversified social actors than [anything that] had ever before existed in American history."[2]

While NIF was not primarily designed or intended for social research, the network does provide, in essence, a laboratory for observing public deliberation and its effects. And what has been tested in this real-life laboratory is, in large part, Dan Yankelovich's theory of public judgment. The experience of this network provides a vantage point for understanding many of the questions Yankelovich posed in *Coming to Public Judgment* about how citizens can work through their initial views on complex public issues; how issues need to be framed for public discussion; how much knowledge people need in order to grapple with complex issues; whether deliberation can accelerate the process of moving through various stages involved in coming to judgment; and whether experts and public officials are prepared to take the outcome of deliberative events seriously. Our intention in this chapter is to reflect on that NIF experience to see what light it may shed on these questions.

Public deliberation, even about matters of urgent importance, is often notable by its absence. Late in 2002, just a few months before President Bush sent troops into Iraq, political scientist Benjamin Barber, writing in *The American Prospect*, commented on the absence of public deliberation about the wisdom of initiating this war, or its likely effects. "As things stand," he wrote, "if the president goes to war, and is likely to go without eliciting either the consent or the dissent, the support or the opposition of the storied American majority, more silent today than ever before at a moment when the raucous contestation of democratic deliberation is desperately needed. . . . We have to admit our own complicity in the outcome that our choices or our disengagement produce."[3]

That complicit silence is what the NIF experiment, started two decades earlier, had set out to address. Over the past twenty-eight years, this community-based network has dealt with America's global role, the health care crisis, poverty in America, the hollowing out of the American middle class, the immigration dilemma, terrorism, energy options, the future of Social Security and Medicare, morally divisive and potentially explosive issues such as abortion, and dozens of other vexing public problems. Deliberations about these issues have provided examples of "the raucous contestation of democratic deliberation." It is worth noting, however, that the tone of most of these forum conversations—notwithstanding momentary heated exchanges—has been surprisingly civil. The impression observers get is of amiable but concerned people who are aware that things are not going well—even, in many cases, that something is genuinely wrong—but who recognize that remedies are within reach.

It is readily apparent when one rereads *Coming to Public Judgment*, some eighteen years after the book was published, that it was propelled, even at the time, by a sense of urgency about fundamental problems of democratic life that were unresolved then and are still more pressing today. As the authors have heard Dan Yankelovich say on various occasions, "You can't run a democracy if it's going to be based on raw opinion." The Kettering Foundation has added to this thought the conviction that you can't run a democracy if it is built only on technical data and professional institutions, while the NIF network has demonstrated that tens of thousands of citizens in communities across the country are prepared to address complex public issues and engage in the serious work of intentional public conversation from which sound judgment may emerge.

A Brief History of the National Issues Forums

In the 1980s, when Dan Yankelovich was first drafting the series of lectures for Syracuse University that would ultimately become his book about public judgment, we were lucky enough to be, bit by bit, as it were, among a trial audience for the thoughts he was shaping. What struck us most forcefully at the time was that despite his astute perceptions of the failings of parties, governments, *and* the public, Yankelovich thought there were progressive steps or stages to the way humans think through important public issues. His idea revealed the patterns of human responses to particular predicaments—and sometimes the extraordinary sophistication and skill in people's evasions of responsibilities.

Among those who came into productive contact with Yankelovich in those years was David Mathews. Even in the relatively mild, brief years of the Ford administration in the mid-1970s, Mathews reports that, as head of the federal government's largest agency, the then Department of Health, Education, and Welfare, he had become more and more concerned about obvious differences between what government sets out to do and what citizens seemed to think important or useful. And when he resumed his presidency of the University of Alabama, that preoccupation led him to invite other educators to join in considering ways to address this apparent weakness in the functioning of our democracy. As president of the Kettering Foundation a few years later, he sought and encouraged other foundation executives to turn their interest toward it as well. Their response was initially not helpful: then, as perhaps now, many foundations thought of their constituencies as institutions rather than individual citizens. Only Deborah Wadsworth, then at the Markle Foundation and later a president of Public Agenda, had words of encouragement: "You should talk with Dan Yankelovich."

While Yankelovich would not publish *Coming to Public Judgment* for another decade, the gaps between public officials and the public, and between policy and the public's understanding, had long commanded his attention. So when he, Mathews, and a few colleagues gathered one morning in the Markle Foundation's conference room in New York City, the seeds of both a concept and an institution were planted.

At the Kettering Foundation, Mathews had already gathered a small group of individuals from academic institutions and not-for-profit organizations, intent on forming what (for want of a better term) they dubbed a "domestic policy association" that would organize public discussions on contemporary issues in communities around the country. Yankelovich, with former Secretary of State Cyrus Vance, had earlier established Public Agenda, where a small group of young professionals had signed on to explore and analyze the ways in which the public approaches—or resists approaching—critical current issues. And the meeting of these two institutions ended with the understanding that, while Public Agenda would seek to frame and present a few critical issues each year in terms that a broad public could readily grasp and respond to, Kettering would encourage nongovernmental, academic, and community groups to engage citizens throughout the country in such discussions, and find ways of communicating their outcomes, essentially to the media and to political leaders, who are thought to be charged with pursuing the public good.

Thus the first three "issue guides" that Public Agenda prepared, in 1982, for use by what became about 150 communities across the country each presented three or four different, if not mutually exclusive, proposals for handling an issue that was currently high on the nation's agenda. The implied presumption was that, after the assembled participants in a local forum had talked together about the competing approaches to an issue and the corresponding drawbacks or trade-offs each entailed, they would make an informed decision about which choice they were ready to follow. All of us who were engaged in the experiment at the time thought that what would emerge from the forums would be an acceptable indicator of a potential public judgment about what *should* be done, sufficiently well thought out— and sufficiently in command of a general public understanding—to be presented as a viable indication of a course of action the nation might confidently follow.

Mass Opinion and Public Judgment: Lessons from the National Issues Forums

Yankelovich notes in *Coming to Public Judgment* that the dominant mode of public discourse in our society is adversarial. Far from encouraging movement toward common ground, adversarial exchanges accentuate differences. As long as that remains the dominant form of discourse—and it does— Yankelovich says, "We're in trouble as a society."

The kind of deliberation we have tried to invite in the National Issues Forums starts with a series of ground rules for this different sort of conversation, whose conditions are laid out in *Coming to Public Judgment*. This alternative form of discourse presumes a willingness to hear differences and the reasons and values behind them. It presumes that all participants are equals, not divided into a hierarchy of experts and amateurs. It presumes that participants are willing to take into account at least the basic information needed to understand what is at stake. It presumes that costs and trade-offs associated with different courses of action have been presented fairly and realistically. It presumes, finally, that in contrast to adversarial, win-lose exchanges such as those the news media feature—especially media outlets that present "news with a view"—participants are willing to reserve judgment in order to move toward an outcome that recognizes points of agreement or common ground. These, says Yankelovich, are crucial requirements for moving to what may be called a public judgment.

But this is a lot to presume. Many skeptics have concluded that it is too much to presume. In part, the National Issues Forums have provided a test of whether anything resembling this ideal can be created and sustained in local forums as citizens grapple with common concerns in their communities and at the national level. There are various ways in which public conversations could be arranged: in the form of debates, public hearings, or juries, for example, or as town meetings that feature question-and-answer sessions with public figures or experts. *Coming to Public Judgment* is in part a how-to manual, a description of how deliberative forums should be designed. But what distinguishes deliberative forums from other kinds of public conversations?

Yankelovich's book describes three features of deliberative forums, each of which is practiced in the National Issues Forums and illustrated in the issue guides that frame forum discussions. The first is "choice work"—that is, considering a series of different perspectives on the issue at hand. The second is framing issues in public terms rather than in expert terms or in the frame of reference of elected officials and policy makers. The third is the role factual information plays in deliberative conversations.

The premise of the deliberative model, as Yankelovich explains it, is that people form judgments by exposing themselves to different perspectives. Deliberation consists of looking at a single issue through different lenses, seeing differences in how people approach it, and, in this way, understanding what advocates of each perspective find important, in the sense of both the key facts that inform their view and the values that underlie it.

Choice Work in Action

In *Coming to Public Judgment*, Yankelovich makes the case that "choice work" is the central element of public deliberation. This is reflected in the issue guides that have been prepared over the years, each consisting of a series of alternative perspectives on a single issue, presented in the voice of its advocates. Typically, we have presented three approaches for each issue, sometimes four, to embrace fundamental values that may prove to be in tension with one another as the options unfold. The focus is on a specific issue, not on personalities or ideological differences. Over the years, as a way to help participants sort out their views without the distraction of party labels and political affiliations, we have made a point of not associating particular perspectives with the president or with party politics in general. While it is impossible to set aside partisan politics entirely, the issue guides and the deliberative conversations are designed, as much as possible, to address different perspectives based on their merits.

For example, a recent issue guide, "The Energy Problem: Choices for an Uncertain Future," offers a brief, nonpartisan statement of the energy challenges the nation faces and then lists three objectives the nation might pursue to come to terms with them:

- Reduce Our Dependence on Foreign Energy
- Get Out of the Fossil Fuel Predicament
- Reduce Our Demand for Energy

By laying out different approaches, the issue guides provide a starting point for forum discussions, with the intention of moving beyond the binary choices that most public exchanges offer. Each approach presents not only the facts that its advocates marshal in support of their views, but also costs and trade-offs that advocates will accept. The intention is to offer an alternative to partisan politics, in which proposals are often presented by advocates who are not forthcoming about the costs and trade-offs inevitably associated with their approach.

We will come back in a moment to these costs and trade-offs and the role they play in helping the public work through its thinking. For now, it is sufficient to mention the intention of explicitly laying out costs and trade-offs, which is to counter the wishful thinking that often colors public thinking, and the ingenuity most people show in downplaying the costs associated with measures they favor.

At a time when proliferating media sources permit people to choose news and commentary that reinforce views they already hold (thus reinforcing the "Daily Me"), deliberative conversations offering alternative perspectives are particularly important. Largely as a result of the Internet, it is increasingly easy for people to tailor the news and opinion they get to their own preconceived views; as a result, the tendency is to live in ideological bubbles, insulated from the views of those who think differently. For that reason, it is more important than ever to create public spaces where a diversity of views can be heard and where people with different views can talk together. One intention of the NIF issue guides is to create such an environment, a framework that acknowledges different perspectives, each of which typically reflects common values that need to be heard if we are to identify shared concerns and common ground.

One fundamental question in political theory is whether citizens are capable of transcending their self-interest and moving toward a conception of the public good, or even capable of listening with an open mind to viewpoints they disagree with. In his prescription for a strong democracy, Ben Barber states the ideal in these words: " 'I will listen' means to the strong democrat, 'I will put myself in his place. I will try to understand. I will strain to hear what makes us alike. I will listen for a common purpose or common good.' "[4] To skeptics who dismiss the possibility that most people are capable of transcending their self-interest, this is a heroic and unrealistic assumption. For those of us who have helped prepare issue guides and moderated forums, listening to alternative perspectives is a necessary and practical step in the deliberative process. Forum moderators are reminded of their obligation to ensure that forums allow each perspective to be taken into consideration and presented with its best foot forward, as an inevitable subject of deliberation. And evidence shows that forum participants are not only perfectly capable but often eager to have this kind of conversation about issues that deeply concern them.

Framing Issues in Public Terms

Yankelovich underlines the importance of another feature of deliberative conversations by pointing to the importance of framing issues in public terms. One of the chief impediments to public deliberation is that issues framed in the media or discussed by public officials tend to be presented in expert terms, not in ways that reflect public perceptions and preoccupations. Sometimes they are presented in the language of public policy, which is closer to the way academics and experts talk than to the way ordinary citizens talk. Media accounts often feature legislative proposals, which bear little resemblance to the way most people think about public problems. Or stories are framed in terms of ideological differences with the presumption that this is how most people think.

In each of these respects, National Issues Forums have taken a different approach, one that reflects the public's preoccupations and concerns. People need to see issues named and framed in ways that reflect their values, their language, and their experience, which are usually quite different from how experts or elected officials approach these problems. Often, as Yankelovich has argued over the years, the public's preoccupations are serious concerns that have gotten too little attention from leadership. Even if those concerns seem trivial or irrelevant to experts and policy makers, they need to be acknowledged if the intention is to bring the public into the conversation.

When longtime National Issues Forums forum conveners like Julie Zimet in El Paso, Texas, say that "we try to avoid experts," her point is not to dismiss experts or their role. It is, rather, to emphasize the distinctive contribution the public makes. It is not only that citizen participants in the forums she convenes don't talk like experts. They don't *think* like experts, either, she says, which leads to a fundamental point about the distinctive value of the public's perspective: an issue commands public attention to the degree that people see or anticipate its impact on their own lives or those of their acquaintances—and genuine public deliberation begins and continues with reflections on experience that is genuine and personal.

Seeing Values as More Important Than Facts and Figures

One long-standing theme in the literature on public engagement in democratic life is a concern that most citizens are poorly informed about public issues. Thus they can hardly be expected to engage in thoughtful conversations about those issues. This was the central point, for example, in Philip Converse's often-quoted study, *The Nature of Belief Systems in Mass Publics*, which concluded that a poorly informed public that has not thought through the issues holds views that are volatile and likely to change.[5] This same concern about public ignorance and the volatility of public opinion fuels the concerns of many skeptics. In his book *The Myth of the Rational Voter*, Bryan Caplan refers to a study he conducted on differences between the views of PhD economists and those of the general public, which showed, not surprisingly, that most Americans do not think like economists.[6] In particular, his concern was that a lack of understanding leads most of the American public to a bias against free markets and the global economy. He concludes that given such irrationality and the extent to which citizens think differently from economists, the voting public cannot be expected to express rational preferences or know what is in its long-term interest. His assertion, like the conclusion of Converse's study, raises a fundamental question that deserves a serious answer: How *can* you engage the public in serious conversation on complex matters about which most people are not well informed?

Yankelovich addresses this question, observing that while information plays an important role in informing public judgment, it is not the most important factor. People do not need to *become* experts to engage in reasonably well-informed discussions. In preparing issue guides on dozens of different topics, one of our objectives has been to present enough information, including key facts and trends, to enable participants to understand the issue. On occasion, a single piece of information that corrects a widely held misunderstanding changes the course of public discussion. This was the case, for example, in National Issues Forums on America's global role, where participants—like most of the American public—at first seriously overestimated the level of U.S. spending on foreign aid. Once participants learned how small a proportion of its overall budget the United States actually spends on foreign aid compared to what other countries spend, the conversation changed.

In general, however, as Yankelovich points out in many places, including the introduction to this volume, the role of information in forming public judgment is overrated. Most experts, like Caplan, believe that people need to know a great deal—in effect, to become experts—in order to participate knowledgeably in public discussion. Our experience in more than twenty-five years of forums suggests otherwise. While it is important to supply participants with the irreducible minimum of key facts and background knowledge on a given issue, these facts can be readily supplied by magazine-length issue guides. What people bring to the discussion themselves, however, in terms of experience and values—these are the real starting points.

And this is Yankelovich's main point: public discussion tends to revolve around values, not facts. Whether the issue is reforming Social Security and Medicare, dealing with the immigration problem, or struggling with how to respond to terrorism, deliberation consists less in bringing facts to bear on decisions, than in aligning people's views with their values. This does not imply that the public is deficient in important ways, as Converse, Caplan, and a long line of skeptics before Caplan have concluded. It is a way of acknowledging what the public adds to the conversation of democracy.

With regard to overall expectations about public deliberation and how it helps people move toward more considered judgments, Yankelovich makes a final, critical point that these forums have frequently illustrated. The word "deliberation," he points out, suggests a rational, orderly, almost academic exercise, as if reason and evidence are the main factors that influence the process of coming to public judgment. In this respect, the word would be misleading. As people come to grips with issues, they are influenced by various factors: personal stories as much as facts, emotion as much as reason. All these factors are involved in the process of "working through."

In a forum on abortion, for example, there was a vivid and deeply personal moment when one woman said, "I can't imagine having an abortion . . . but then, I did." In a forum on welfare policy, a woman's story about her dependence on welfare checks visibly swayed the group. Far from being irrelevant distractions, personal stories and experiences play an important role in helping participants see all sides of the public problems they are addressing and the human dilemmas behind them.

The expectation that public deliberation should resemble exchanges among experts misses the point. Citizens are not experts. Even when they are reasonably well informed, they shouldn't be expected to think like experts. The point of public deliberation is to talk together about overall principles and priorities of public action. These, finally, are judgment calls about what should be done, matters in which no one has special expertise or a privileged position, matters that are properly informed by public conversation.

"Working Through"

In *Coming to Public Judgment*, Yankelovich presents a schema depicting successive stages for "working through" a difficult choice, from "dawning awareness" to "greater urgency" and "wishful thinking" to "weighing the choices" and "taking a stand." These steps can be used, he says, as a way to reckon the characteristics of the public's thinking and distinguish between early-stage mushiness or volatility and the more stable characteristics of a carefully weighed public judgment. The experience of the National Issues Forums sheds light on the process that Yankelovich refers to as "working through" but also reveals the deliberative process we have observed in forum discussions subtly enriching the linear, or "step-wise," sequence he describes in his book.

With respect to the various issues the NIF series have considered over the past quarter century, both the issue guides and the forum moderators have explicitly laid out costs and trade-offs to generate a realistic assessment of the consequences of a given course of action. The question for forum participants—and for the public as a whole—is whether people are willing to support a particular course of action when they grasp its costs and trade-offs.

A forum in Pittsburgh, for example, considered whether expensive medical assistance should be provided to a relatively young family member, who seemed unlikely to benefit from it in the long run. The deliberation was both clear and compelling because the group focused on a real-life example presented by one of the participants, a young widower. Responding to the painful emotions associated with the dilemma, most participants struggled before acknowledging that hard choices would be necessary, weighing the costs they might have to bear against a sense of loss they could genuinely understand.

"Working through," as we have seen it taking place in various forums, is an apt metaphor. It describes an important aspect of public deliberation, as people face difficult choices in public life, resisting and struggling in various ways with the implications. In doing so they express a variety of reactions, including denial, anger, and disbelief, before they finally move—often sympathetically and together—toward accepting the realities.

If citizens have not considered the costs or likely consequences of a course of action, they are likely to experience anger, denial, or "sticker shock" when confronted with the downsides. In such cases they may frequently change their mind—or sharply decrease their support for certain views.

In *Coming to Public Judgment*, Yankelovich clearly implies a progressive logic in the way people think about public issues, describing the stepwise stages as occurring in a more or less predictable sequence. What we have seen in the forums, however, takes a somewhat different form. Public deliberation does not typically proceed in a linear way. More tango than foxtrot, deliberation tends to be characterized by hesitations, cross-steps, and reversal of course. Nonetheless, it is progressive. Recognizable strains of thought have beginnings, middles, and ends. One leads to the next, or at least gives rise to it. Thus the understandings that deliberative forums ultimately arrive at are more widely shared than the individual opinions voiced at the beginning.

Toward a Typology of Deliberative Conversations

Our analysis of videotaped forums reviewed and condensed over sixteen years for the PBS television series *Public Voice* shows a sequence of recognizable kinds of conversations that are apparent in deliberation at different stages. Together, these conversational "stages" facilitate the process of coming to public judgment. First, people voice their opinions, often in personal stories. This slow and rather circuitous sharing of personal understandings of the issue is a way of talking about the underlying problem, naming it, and describing its essence. The stories are highly individual, often reflecting quite different and even contradictory perspectives. People don't yet have answers. They do not yet agree on how to name and frame the issue. What emerges from this phase of the conversation, however, is a more broadly shared recognition of common concerns.

At this stage, the issue guide and the approaches it describes serve not as a fixed menu of options for participants but rather as diverse points of entry, contrasting perspectives on how to name the problem. Often a common sense of the issue does not arise until midway through the forum. Even then, some participants circle back to previously shared stories and perspectives that are not shared, to suggest subtle modifications in what may be an embryonic "shared" opinion.

What follows are narratives of accumulated understanding, generated as people try to comprehend the complexity of the issue as it has been revealed and discussed. In this phase, each new story or perspective requires participants to reframe and often expand their own perspectives. A kind of aggregated story thus emerges that represents a shared understanding of the problem, although it is still a long way from a coherent collective judgment about what should be done.

The comprehensive narrative that arises nevertheless does begin to take the shape of a shared understanding; it is a collective creation. Recognized in this sense, deliberation does not consist of "choices" demanding a judgment or the measured weighing of trade-offs. Rather, deliberation consists of aggregating perceptions shared to the point where most participants feel they have a complete story, though its moral may be unclear when applied to individual instances.

This sequence is what we experienced in forums on the topic of immigration, for example. In their early stages, the conversations covered a lot of ground. Before participants were ready to address the question of what should be done about immigration policy, many views and stories were exchanged—sometimes circling back to what had already been said—about the implications of being a "nation of immigrants." What was said initially in many forums amounted to a deepening of the collective understanding about the dilemmas implied in that promise. In this early phase, participants seemed to come to a clearer understanding of what mattered most to them about immigration—its individual and collective importance—and then to wrestle with the ambiguities and contradictions often associated with the arrival of immigrants into a settled community. The authors observed one guest commentator at the *Public Voice* taping on the immigration issue at the National Press Club in Washington characterize what he saw in the following words: "This conversation should offer us hope . . . about the American public. It's a very complicated issue. It's riddled with contradictions in people's values. What we saw in these tapes today was the American public's ability and willingness to engage, to wrestle with these challenges, and try to figure out, with the information they have, how we might be able to move forward."

What seemed to happen in the course of these forums, in other words, was the emergence of a pattern of thinking over time, a process of change as participants considered other people's experiences and ways of thinking. Although in many cases opinions did not change, people's understanding of the costs and consequences of different courses of action did change—and so, too, did their understanding of why others' opinions differed from their own.

A Case Study in Deliberation: The Energy Issue

The energy issue—a multifaceted concern that includes global warming, energy self-sufficiency, environmental threats, and security issues—provides a revealing recent example of the importance of public deliberation and the challenge of helping citizens move toward public judgment. The issue, first recognized as a serious national concern during the Carter administration in the late 1970s, has disappeared and reappeared at various points since then, each time in a somewhat different guise. The recent combination of record-high gas prices (which persisted until the late summer of 2008), growing wariness about U.S. dependence on foreign oil, abnormal weather patterns, and agreement that the threat of global warming was real pushed energy to near the top of the nation's worry list.

When you combine these facets of public awareness and concern, as Yankelovich has often noted, it is apparent that the American public is in a different place today from where it had been earlier. Recent events such as the massive oil spill in the Gulf of Mexico have pushed the public beyond its initial and muddled awareness of the issue into a stage of urgent concern. The question now, as legislators consider various measures to deal with the problem, is whether the public is ready to support the costs and trade-offs associated with such proposals. Because this is such a demanding issue, NIF discussions of the nation's energy options that took place late in 2007 and early 2008 provide a revealing case study in the use of public deliberation, toward accomplishing what Yankelovich envisioned in *Coming to Public Judgment*.

In the course of preparing for the *Public Voice* television program, which aired nationally on PBS stations in 2007, we reviewed videotapes of forums in five communities. Together these forums—each lasting about two hours—provide a snapshot of public deliberation on the energy issue, a glimpse of how people were weighing what should be done in the face of an increasingly urgent national problem. These forums revealed a public trying to address a challenge that demands speedy action and imposes costs and sacrifices that will have to be agreed on and shared.

In these forums, there was conversation about energy-intensive lifestyles; about conservation measures that we might adopt individually and collectively; about missed opportunities over the years to adjust our habits and develop new kinds of energy supplies; and about the growing hazard of depending on unreliable international suppliers for our energy lifeline in a context of increasing competition worldwide—all the while putting off key decisions and remaining dependent on oil and other carbon-based fuel sources. The tone of the deliberations was not grim—NIF community gatherings seldom are—but it was serious.

In these forums, people from very different kinds of communities in New Hampshire, New York, Ohio, Oregon, and Texas confronted the reality of a crisis, for which they blamed themselves, corporate interests, and their political leaders. Many participants raised the issue of American self-indulgence to explain why the United States has been slow to take serious, disciplined action. Then, although with some initial reluctance, there was a gradual acceptance and finally a groundswell of support for the view that Americans need government to take a firm leadership role, as it had done in developing the Manhattan Project that produced the first atomic bomb— an example that was cited in several different locations, as though it were a remembered experience. What at first was mentioned by just a few participants became over the course of the discussions a refrain: Why doesn't government act decisively to ensure the public interest by taking a leadership role and enacting laws that would serve as incentives and restraints? This was the gist of what seemed to be sometimes a puzzled and sometimes an angry question.

People had typically started these discussions with familiar but differing views about such matters as which alternative energy sources seem most promising; and in many cases personal opinions in these matters did not appear to change much in the discussions. Participants nervous about nuclear power seemed little comforted by the knowledge that Europe depends on it or by the fact that a significant amount of power in the United States already comes from nuclear plants; participants concerned about the preservation of wildlife and wilderness in the United States remained unwilling to sacrifice it for what would still be diminishing oil resources. What did coalesce, however, was a sense of shared values and certain common understandings about the possibility of tolerable potential public action.

People who began by griping about the price of gasoline (while acknowledging that they were doing little to change their own oil-dependent habits) seemed to achieve, in most cases, a collective sensibility by the time these deliberations concluded. The underlying sense—expressed in the frequent references to the Manhattan Project and to the Marshall Plan (which helped revive a devastated Europe after World War II)—of a desire and need to accomplish something collectively recurred with increasing insistence in these forums to take the form, finally, of citizens who slowly began to frame what they thought *should* happen. Recognizing that no one acting alone can accomplish much, and that without collective agreement (and perhaps a little coercion) few people are likely to change their energy-using habits, they called on government and elected officials to perform their role. As one man in a Texas forum put it, "We understand the crisis. Now it's up to you to lead us."

In March 2008, a jury of distinguished panelists, including experts, journalists, and leaders of several nonprofit research organizations, met at a public event in Washington to examine what took place in these forums, using Yankelovich's stages as a template to assess the state of public thinking about energy. First, they asked whether participants in deliberative forums agreed on the urgency of the issue and shared a general sense of what should be done. That was fairly easy to answer. Forum participants were, or became, well aware of at least some of the ways energy problems affect them, especially direct effects such as the price of home heating oil and the price of gas at the pump. They readily acknowledged that global progress would mark an end to "cheap oil" in the United States. And they were not indifferent to the environmental dangers of fossil fuels. As they deliberated, forum participants became increasingly convinced of the urgent need for public action.

Second, comparing public thinking and experts' views, the jurors asked themselves how successfully the participants had grasped or framed the complexity of the issue. There was less agreement about the ability of forum participants to put the pieces of the energy problem together. One or two panel members commented that, even after a few hours of deliberative conversations, forum participants still viewed the issue in a compartmentalized fashion. But the sense of the jury as a whole, including its journalists and organizational leaders, was that the forum participants had brought together aspects of the energy problem too often separated (they said) by special interests.

Finally, the jurors tried to assess whether forum participants had been realistic in assessing the options for public action—and how close they might be to grasping the consequences of the actions they seemed to favor. What was readily apparent, judging from what had been presented to those in the Washington gathering, was the inclination of many forum participants to blame corporations for their predicament and voice mistrust about whether government intends to do anything about it. But panelists recognized, too, that forum participants had a serious awareness of—if no ready formula for—the substantial changes that will have to be effected in traditional American lifestyles.

On the one hand, there were repeated expressions of support for government initiatives to encourage energy conservation and to develop alternative energy sources. While forum participants wrestled with the choices and pondered what costs and consequences they would be willing to accept, they did not get to a point of resolution. What seemed clear in the forums was that many people were reluctant to make direct personal sacrifices until they were convinced that others—including oil companies and large corporate interests, as well as fellow citizens—would do their part. As one panelist in the Washington meeting put it, "We're going to have to have a lot more public dialogue to get ourselves in a position to move toward acceptable solutions."

What Have We Learned?

Toward the end of *Coming to Public Judgment*, Yankelovich speculates about what would happen if institutional arrangements were made to practice deliberative democracy in many communities. If we were to "expand the notion of citizen choice now confined to elections to include making choices on the vital issues that confront us every day," he asks, "and if America were to give a high priority to public judgment . . . in what ways would our society and culture be different?"[7]

The Kettering Foundation's main mission is to carry out research about public life, and in the twenty-eight years since the first season of the National Issues Forums, its activities have been examined by a number of researchers at the Kettering Foundation and elsewhere. As a result of this research, we can offer at least a tentative answer to the questions Yankelovich posed by looking at the impact of deliberative public forums on individuals and communities.

Over the years, many advocates of deliberative democracy—from Alexis de Tocqueville in the nineteenth century to contemporary political scientists such as Jane Mansbridge—have regarded deliberation as a school for citizenship. Taking part in deliberation, they claim, changes people in important ways. While we do not have the research base to track long-term changes in individuals who have repeatedly taken part in such forums, we can make some observations about their impact on individual participants.

We can note, for example, that while participation in individual forums does not quickly or dramatically change people's views on the issue at hand, it does alter views in at least one subtle but significant way. What changes are people's perceptions of those with whom they disagree. On various issues, forum participants have acknowledged that they come to understand and appreciate views they do not themselves hold. That modification helps create an opening so that common ground—a broadly acceptable direction for public action—can be identified. A closely related finding is this:

by joining in deliberative events and interacting with people they do not ordinarily talk to, participants report that their outlook is broadened. Anecdotal evidence from Cincinnati, Dayton, and other communities indicates that participation in a wider circle of conversation about race relations, for example, helped expand social networks and broaden people's perspectives.

Beyond that, people become more confident that what they say matters and are more willing to listen to those with different perspectives. The experience thus not only enhances their sense of involvement but also their sense of self-efficacy. Moreover, participation in forums strengthens people's motivation to seek out additional issue-related information and take part in other public activities. Almost inevitably, it seems—and this is fundamental in the movement toward public judgment—participation in deliberative forums helps participants move beyond initial preferences to more stable and internally consistent views.

In summary, then, studies of the impact of NIF discussions on individuals show various kinds of effects that, when considered as a whole, are significant. Regarding the impact on communities, it is clear that the *habit* of holding deliberative events to address public concerns helps bolster confidence that communities *can* respond when common concerns or problems arise. Some of the memorable moments in this series of forums have involved efforts to create a civil atmosphere for talking about highly charged issues, including abortion and race. In Owensboro, Kentucky, despite initial misgivings on the part of many participants, forums on race provided a civil setting for talking about interracial relations. Those forums succeeded in raising awareness among whites about the lack of trust experienced by many African Americans.

Many communities have reported similar experiences. In Grand Rapids, Michigan, for example, a community long familiar with racial tensions, forums have been convened for more than two decades, and the experience of repeated deliberative events has affected the way the community responds to new problems. Kettering researchers who compared different processes for bringing citizens and elected officials together in Grand Rapids concluded that collaborative forms of deliberation may be the most fruitful over the long run because they transform the way citizens and officeholders practice politics. This is not to say that deliberation is a cure-all, or that the forums practiced in the NIF network invariably lead participants directly to something resembling public judgment. But it is certainly a robust response to skeptics who tend to dismiss the idea of deliberative forums as a fantasy that makes unrealistic assumptions about the political attitudes of normal citizens and their capacity and willingness to engage in public choices.

Among the rules for successful deliberation laid out in *Coming to Public Judgment*, one in particular is worth revisiting. Yankelovich's Rule Four is that you have to give the public the incentive of knowing that someone is listening to what happens in deliberative forums, and take measures to ensure that leaders take the outcome of these events into account. This rule relates to one of the book's central themes—the gap that separates the public and elected officials, and the uncomfortable fact that public opinion and the thinking of policy makers often seem to be worlds apart.

This is obviously a practical and important concern. People who participate in these forums want the outcome of their conversations to be taken seriously by elected officials and policy makers. People participate in the hard work of deliberative forums because they want more of a say in decisions that will affect them, as people, and they don't want deliberative forums to be dismissed as "mere talk." The hope and expectation are that the kind of public deliberation exemplified by National Issues Forums will, over time, become an integral part of democratic decision making.

Those of us who have worked with the NIF network for more than two decades have participated in various efforts to collate what comes out of forums and communicate it to various groups at the local and national level. The Kettering Foundation, working in collaboration with the NIF network, has helped prepare annual summary reports, based on questionnaires and narrative descriptions from forums around the country. But most reporters—and perhaps many political leaders—do not know what to make of deliberative events, so it may be relatively easy for elected officials to dismiss forums as unrepresentative or atypical. That the forums represent the thoughts and feelings of people who have taken the time to think through issues as they relate to their own lives and values, and to talk about them in community meetings, is not a virtue that is readily apparent to many public officials. There are notable exceptions, including communities in which elected officials recognize the unique value of forums and regularly take part in them. But even after twenty-eight years, this network is still not widely recognized, nor are outcomes of deliberative forums widely consulted by elected officials as a gauge of the considered judgment of the American public.

Sociologists Carmen Sirianni and Lewis Friedland, in their account of the deliberative democracy movement, write that NIF and other organizations have made impressive strides in "renovating the democratic foundations of American society, and creating forms of civic practice that are far more sophisticated in grappling with complex public problems." They go on to say, however, that "these important foundational accomplishments should not be exaggerated, nor the obstacles to further development of a broad movement underestimated."[8]

At a time when an increasing number of media outlets present "news with a view," and at a time when many Americans live in ideological enclaves of like-minded people, it is particularly important to have public spaces where different values and views are heard, and where those with different opinions listen to each other and, over time, move toward a collective "public judgment." To this end, therefore, since its inception, NIF has made a series of efforts to be rigorously nonpartisan. And after twenty-eight years of helping to prepare issue guides for this network, we are still struck by the continuing challenge of naming and framing issues so that they reflect a wide range of voices in the public debate and are not biased for or against any of them.

In various ways—in the framing of issues, perhaps, or the slant of a local moderator—the efforts of this network could easily tilt toward one or another partisan or ideological position. If that were to happen, the network would quickly attract like-minded people and chase away those with different values and views, and the entire effort would quickly lose most of its value. Advocacy groups are readily found, but developing and sustaining a nonpartisan network that provides a public space for many voices and values remains a challenge.

Public Judgment and the Practice of Democracy

When Americans talk about democracy, they think primarily about the formal procedures and institutions of governance and, in particular, about what elected officials do. What tends to be overlooked and not well understood is what citizens do: their role in a democratic process that speaks, after all, in their name. To some of us, therefore, one profoundly valuable contribution that Dan Yankelovich's *Coming to Public Judgment* makes is to shed light on the public's conversation and its relation to the formal process of governance, and on the distinction between opinion and "public judgment" that gives the book its name.

Deliberative forums along the lines Yankelovich laid out—what the NIF network has done for almost three decades—are not a cure-all for what is wrong with democratic governance in the United States today. These forums, however, and the light they throw on the process of reaching a judgment that is collective genuinely represent an important contribution to our understanding of the democratic process. If, as Yankelovich said, "you can't run a democracy if it is going to be based on raw opinion," it is no small achievement to show how we can move toward public judgment.

When Yankelovich joined with Cyrus Vance to establish Public Agenda, and when soon after they joined with David Mathews and the Kettering Foundation to help create the National Issues Forums, the purpose of their joint effort was to enable political leadership to better serve the public interest. The concept of public judgment is a way of reckoning the current characteristics of public thinking, a way of understanding what needs to be done to help people move forward in *their own* understanding. Now, almost twenty years after its publication, we value Yankelovich's book because it celebrates public judgment and recognizes its crucial importance to the polity. The challenge for Public Agenda, the Kettering Foundation, the National Issues Forums, Viewpoint Learning, and other groups engaged in learning about the public is to understand and illuminate the obstructions to public judgment, and in this way help cultivate the habits and civic actions necessary for democracy to work.

As Yankelovich points out in his book, and as we have consistently noted in our research about public deliberation, there is a fundamental difference between public opinion and the kinds of public judgments people reach in the course of deliberation. What public deliberation gives us is not a more detailed version of what opinion polls provide, which is to tell elected officials precisely what they should do. Nor does deliberation, as we have seen it, represent a formally agreed-upon judgment in the form of some sort of consensus statement. The goal of deliberative forums, as we have come to understand them through NIF, is to illuminate why people support certain courses of action and what their reservations and main concerns are. As Yankelovich says, public judgment sets "the boundaries of public permission." Through our deliberations as a people, we delineate the life that we, as a people, want to live.

What we can report from forums is not primarily the specific policies that a majority of Americans favor, what middle-of-the-road compromise is likely to garner broad support, or what a majority of Americans believe. On given issues public deliberation may shed some light on each of these matter. The main contribution of public judgment is that it leads to the discovery of what we have in common. It reveals the concerns and priorities that public policy should reflect, and it sheds light on *why* they are important.

In a culture that tends to think of "government of, by, and for the people" as a process mainly carried out by elected representatives who, once chosen, don't need much direction from the publics they represent, it is not conventional to think of a deliberative public as setting the terms within which policy makers should operate. And yet, finally, this is what public deliberation and its outcome, public judgment, have to contribute, and what we have seen it contribute in National Issues Forums and the communities that host them. If NIF and related citizen deliberation processes have not succeeded in transforming the national political culture—and certainly they have not—they have at least demonstrated that a deliberative public is a viable possibility. More than that, they have helped bring about such deliberative publics in many communities across the nation, which is surely a critical step, possibly *the* critical step, toward a more deeply democratic national politics.

The vital word in *Coming to Public Judgment*, it seems, is "coming." It is in the process of *coming* to judgment that the public exercises its sovereignty. The stages that Yankelovich identified are not markers on a ruler, a way of judging deficiencies in the public's thinking. Nor, taken together, do they function like a congressional whip, demanding a vote on predetermined legislation. The kinds of thinking associated with Yankelovich's various stages are not necessarily experienced in a given sequence or by every citizen at the same time. The beauty of coming to public judgment is that it is the practice of democracy itself, the means by which genuine democracy is intended to work.

CHAPTER 4

Thirty-Five Years of Working on Public Judgment at Public Agenda

ALISON KADLEC AND WILL FRIEDMAN

Beginnings

Public Agenda was founded by Dan Yankelovich and Cyrus Vance in 1975 as a kind of democracy project aimed at infusing the policy process with a much richer approach to public opinion than had previously existed. In this chapter, we reflect on Public Agenda's efforts over the years to put this perspective into practice in order to inform policy making, strengthen communities and their vital institutions, and educate and empower citizens. Our hope is that these reflections will yield insights useful to the work of policy makers, thought leaders, civil society organizations, public engagement practitioners, and deliberative democracy researchers and theorists.

Yankelovich's new approach to public opinion research was, in its own way, a subversive enterprise. In the traditional relationship between leaders and the public, policy is a matter for elites, created out of a dance among experts, interest group leaders, and public officials. There may be some polling to inform "strategic communication" aimed at the public. But rarely in this policy mode are citizens truly included. Rather, leaders use polling in an attempt to gauge how big a management problem the public is likely to be with respect to a given issue, and to gain competitive advantage by claiming to represent them.

Yankelovich created a unique approach to public opinion, unlike anything pollsters, and the leaders they sought to inform, had encountered. According to Deborah Wadsworth, former president of Public Agenda, "At the core of [Yankelovich's] thinking is a deep respect for the public [that] allowed him to zero in on the idea that if you could reframe issues in the public's language, you could identify the public's stage of understanding and its capacity to learn and think about difficult issues under the right conditions."[1] This approach challenged the notion that citizens must have expert-level information in order to make good judgments, and it informed policy making by clarifying the public's position on tricky public issues.[2] Perhaps most importantly, Yankelovich's innovative approach highlighted the gaps between leaders and the citizenry, which he argued must be negotiated over time in order for policy to stand on a solid foundation of public understanding and support.

In our opinion research, the principles developed in *Coming to Public Judgment* compel us to ask whether members of the public have done much thinking about an issue, and encourage us to consider survey results in this light. How much "working through" underlies what we're hearing from citizens? Have they faced up to the trade-offs involved in school vouchers or welfare reform, or are their responses more of a first-blush reaction? Are their positions anchored in deep-seated values, or are they reflections of the shifting cable news/talk radio panorama?

The *Coming to Public Judgment* perspective has also been a natural launchpad for direct work with citizens, because it underscores the importance of creating opportunities and tools (such as nonpartisan issue guides) that help them sort through conflicting interests and perspectives. With these ideas animating the organization, Public Agenda emerged as a new kind of nonpartisan intermediary dedicated to bridging the divides between the public and its leaders and to promoting a more democratic understanding of the place of the citizenry in the policy process.[3]

What was clear from the start was that generating meaningful knowledge about the public's attitudes had to proceed on two mutually informing tracks. On the one hand, research could help gauge where the public was on a given issue, in order to understand people's starting point on that issue—their current concerns and preferences—always with an eye on the degree to which the public had worked through the issue and how stable and deeply rooted their positions were. On the other hand, the research identified obstacles and aids relevant to the public's ongoing process of working through and learning, and thus became a basis for finding ways to help citizens engage issues in a meaningful way.

From Reporting on Public Attitudes and Judgment
to Facilitating "Working Through"

One way in which Public Agenda became involved in actively supporting public judgment early in its history was by partnering with the Kettering Foundation and its National Issues Forums initiative. As noted in the previous chapter, Public Agenda's role for many years was to create the issue guides that informed NIF sessions in communities across the nation.[4]

Then there were a number of early Public Agenda projects that directly tested the concepts that Yankelovich articulated in *Coming to Public Judgment*, such as the eye-opening 1988 study on public attitudes toward U.S.–Soviet relations.[5] This innovative research revolved around four alternative U.S.–Soviet "futures." It showed that, when given the proper conditions and balanced information, ordinary citizens were quite able and willing to engage complex issues in thoughtful ways and generate sound, consistent judgment beyond what standard public opinion polls were suggesting at the time.

The study was especially illuminating because it revealed unexpected areas of consensus between liberals and conservatives on Cold War issues that had been obscured by media depictions of hostile, partisan rhetoric. The outcomes of this study suggested that there were even areas where the public was actually *ahead* of leadership in terms of its openness to creative diplomacy and possibilities for peace-building relations. This report not only gave leaders a sense of the values and ideas that the public was bringing to the table on this issue, but it also helped show leaders that they, in fact, had public permission to lead in new ways.

The application of the *Coming to Public Judgment* perspective directly to communities began to emerge as a central focus during the early to mid-1990s. At the time, the organization was having a substantial impact on education reform debates through research that identified gaps between the priorities and thinking of the public and those of leaders, as well as signs that the public's commitment to public schools as a critical public institution was weakening.[6] At around the same period, we began running into more and more school leaders (e.g., superintendents and state education commissioners) who were becoming interested in innovative public engagement approaches to strengthening relationships with the families and communities they served—rather than relying only on traditional public relations strategies for managing media relations and bond votes, which just weren't working anymore. This was, of course, part of a wider phenomenon of a growing skepticism on the part of citizens toward authorities of various stripes that had been gaining steam for decades along with a growing demand for a voice in public affairs, and it was part of a broader response to these dynamics as the study of deliberative democracy deepened in academia, innovative community-based practices began to emerge on a variety of fronts, and the concept of broad-based public engagement gained more currency.[7]

As a result, we developed a major initiative to create dialogue tools for communities to help the general public, local educators, and community leaders communicate more effectively, negotiate differences, and build a foundation of common ground for reform efforts. This project, carried out in partnership with the Institute for Educational Leadership, included a major research report, *Assignment Incomplete*, which identified areas ripe for community dialogue and deliberation; Choicework Discussion Starter materials (print and video) on six education topics; the research, development, and piloting of our "Community Conversation" dialogue process that would apply the materials in public forums in ten pilot sites chosen through a national application process; and, finally, the evaluation and refinement of the methods and materials developed throughout the project.

In contrast to our occasional engagement projects of the past, this initiative set out for the first time an integrated set of public engagement tools and procedures that would have "legs"—that is, approaches that could be refined and tested in communities over time to help citizens work through difficult issues and make headway on a common agenda. Soon, new projects began to evolve rather quickly, including statewide public engagement initiatives on education reform in Nebraska and Connecticut, a partnership with the National Education Association to help create the NEA's Public Engagement Project, and a national initiative with the Public Education Network on race and education.

In 1997, Will Friedman, then associate director of research, established the public engagement department, and since then the public engagement team has built on that early work by creating more than twenty Choicework Discussion Starters on youth and education topics, police–community relations, statewide tax reform, the environment and climate change, the national debt, and urban planning, and by working on scores of public engagement initiatives involving hundreds of communities.

Public Engagement and Public Consultation

Many approaches to deliberative democratic work are primarily concerned with representing the public's thoughts, values, and reflections in the policy debate so that leaders can take them into account as they go about the business of governance. This might be best understood as a *public consultation* mode of working, and it is the dominant framework behind both *Coming to Public Judgment* and the early days of Public Agenda. Such a perspective is reflected in *Coming to Public Judgment's* implicit theory of change, which is to let opinion evolve into judgment and then let policy reflect and be guided by this new context of opinion.

Such a theory of change depends, to a great extent, on the democratic goodwill of leaders or the power of media to compel leaders to pay attention. This approach can be extremely valuable, and a good deal of our work at Public Agenda continues in this vein today. But we find that this framework alone is limiting, and we view it as only one of several approaches to making public deliberation politically meaningful.

By contrast, what we call a *public engagement* framework, while typically including strong elements of public consultation, also involves a broader approach that derives from a more complex theory of change. The principal focus is on strengthening community capacity for boundary-crossing dialogue, deliberation, and collaboration so that many kinds of formal and informal local leaders (and not just public officials) become better able to build a common agenda for change, and so that citizens themselves can not only inform leaders but also work alongside them to address tough public challenges.

Such work is most effective as an iterative, multilevel process that creates conditions for citizens, local leaders, and organizations to not only work *through* issues but also actively work *on* them. By this we mean that we view our work as doing more than offering the public a chance to provide input to leaders. We also view it as a means to develop the ability of multiple community actors to work together on needed solutions.

Strengthening Capacity as the Heart and Soul of the Work

"Capacity building" is a phrase tossed around with increasing frequency in the deliberative democracy field. For us, it refers to efforts aimed *at embedding public engagement practices in the problem-solving culture of a community* in ways that allow for thoughtful, sustained, and active public involvement. In short, to have a lasting impact, public engagement must move beyond "one-and-done" consultative events, and beyond the "project" phase, to become a set of attitudes and practices integrated into the institutions and culture of a community.

Interestingly, this orientation to the work has as much in common with community organizing traditions as with the public consultation mode of deliberative democracy. Like community organizing, a public engagement approach focuses on helping ordinary citizens and community-based organizations work together in new ways, helping historically marginalized groups gain a stronger voice in public decision making, and fostering cooperation among "grass tips" leaders, formal community-based organizations, and informal networks and associations. All of this becomes part of the work, along with the more traditional deliberative democratic work of providing public officials with insights that inform policies and institutional practices.

This mode of working sensitizes practitioners to structural power relations and inequities in ways that doing a bit of research or facilitating a single forum event cannot. It's the difference between doing a focus group or organizing a forum *for* a community and then reporting the results to leaders versus working *with* local leaders to convene stakeholders and organize post-forum action and impacts. In the latter case, the challenges a community faces in bringing about needed change become painfully apparent, as some hopes are invariably dashed even as some possibilities for progress may open up.

This does not mean we then become community organizers and focus our efforts on mobilizing marginalized groups to correct power imbalances. To be clear, we think such work can often be critical to the cause of justice; we just don't see it as the function of a nonpartisan intermediary organization dedicated to broad-based engagement and problem solving. Mobilization campaigns often have a specific goal in mind and a strong legal dimension—for example, ending the illegal exploitation of low-wage workers. Public engagement, on the other hand, is aimed at helping a community develop the practices and habits of including diverse stakeholders in decision making and collaborative problem solving on any issue.

Some community activists and democratic theorists argue that the sort of engagement we promote is pointless so long as significant inequalities prevail in our public life. By contrast, we believe that public engagement—if well designed—can not only be meaningful in spite of power asymmetries but is in fact one important way of fostering more equality of opportunity in society. As we argue at length elsewhere, the seemingly mundane details of design and process can make a tremendous difference in either reproducing or neutralizing pernicious power relations in any given deliberative event or initiative.[8] While we are not naive about the impact of long-standing and deeply entrenched hierarchies of privilege and subordination on public deliberation, our experience tells us that careful design processes and recruitment strategies can help level the playing field and allow a wide range of historically marginalized voices to participate effectively in decision making and problem solving in their communities.

Citizen Choicework Community Conversations: A Method of Facilitating Public Judgment, Community Action, and Civic Learning

Public Agenda's Citizen Choicework Community Conversation model was first piloted in 1996 for a project with the Institute for Educational Leadership (described earlier). It is now a core methodology used in hundreds of communities across the country on dozens of issues. Its dual goals are to promote public deliberation and problem solving on a specific issue while also strengthening the long-term civic capacity of communities to address difficult issues in deliberative ways. Here's how it works.

A Preliminary Phase of Listening Sets the Stage

Every community has its own challenges, assets, history, and way of getting things done. That being the case, we always look to gain a sense of the political context in which a Community Conversation will take place and adjust its application accordingly. For instance, in our work in the Kansas City region on science, technology, and math education (which we'll discuss in greater depth later in this chapter), we had to adapt the Community Conversation work to take several factors into account:

- The need to improve science, technology, engineering, and math (STEM) education was much more salient to local leaders and employers than it was to parents and students.
- There were already many organizations with STEM education on their agenda, some of whom might feel intruded on by "outsiders" unless we were careful in how we introduced our methods and assistance.
- Many community residents and organizational leaders felt "meetinged out" and had had some negative experiences with previous dialogue initiatives.

Simply introducing a forum methodology, no matter how well intended and designed, would be of limited use and could even backfire if we failed to carefully consider these dynamics.

For this reason, a preliminary period of listening, learning, and adapting to the realities on the ground is always a good idea, which is why we typically begin our work with a phase of qualitative (and occasionally quantitative) research. In this step we aim to get a sense of the community's starting point on the issue at hand, the language people use and respond to, the relationship between the public and leaders on the issue, and any adjustment that may be needed in our tools and materials so they'll fit well with the local situation.

A Local, Nonpartisan Planning Team,
Not Public Agenda, Owns the Process

Public Agenda does not, by itself, convene public dialogue or organize public engagement initiatives in communities. How could the results be integral to the life of the community if the discussion had no local roots? There are, therefore, no "Public Agenda forums." Instead, we work with local organizations and leaders to improve collaboration and engage with citizens in their community through locally "branded" tools and processes that we help them adapt to their purposes.

The first order of business, then, is the establishment of a local, nonpartisan or multipartisan coalition to sponsor, organize, and act on the public engagement process, with Public Agenda's role being to provide strategic guidance, training, tools and materials, and other forms of technical assistance. Typically, one or two key local players act as the initial catalysts and the first members of a diverse, local sponsoring coalition and planning team, with representation from a wide range of local community entities. Most join because they have a stake in the issue at hand and are convinced that a successful Community Conversation will help them move their organization forward. Others sometimes join because they believe greater community engagement is important in its own right, whatever the issue, and they are eager to "import" new tools and know-how into their community.

For instance, if the issue at hand concerns workforce development, Public Agenda might help local partners build a planning team that includes groups such as the K–12 school system, local employers or chambers of commerce, community colleges, the mayor's office, community-based organizations (CBOs) that work with the under- and unemployed, and other CBOs such as local churches, community centers, the United Way, or the League of Women Voters. This helps ensure from the outset that a broad cross section of interests will be included in planning, implementation, and follow-up action. Making special efforts to encourage local partners to reach past their comfort zones to include organizations that they have not worked with before can lead to new partnerships that endure long after a round of Community Conversation work has ended.

The Model Is Designed to Foster
Productive Dialogue, Action, and Learning

Elements of design in community forums can determine whether they are sufficiently inclusive, legitimate, productive, and empowering to serve as meaningful points of departure for collaborative work. In this section, we'll discuss several important design components, beginning with how issues are presented to enhance problem-solving dialogue among diverse groups.

Framing for Deliberation. Helping the public come to terms with issues means making them as accessible as possible to as many people as possible, without oversimplifying them to the point of pablum. In our Community Conversation work, we've tried to attend to this need by, whenever possible, using qualitative research to explore the natural language nonexperts use to talk about an issue and the values they bring to it. In the example of STEM education mentioned earlier, this meant downplaying the issue's importance to America's international competitiveness (which experts often emphasize) and paying more attention to the importance of these subjects for opening up career opportunities in the twenty-first-century job market (which parents and students are especially attuned to).

We also use focus groups to test and refine different ways of presenting the issue for dialogue and deliberation prior to "going public." It is particularly challenging to create presentations that make it possible for everyone to participate effectively in discussions where some have a good deal more expertise than others. A "choice work" presentation that provides a concise nonpartisan introduction to an issue along with the pros and cons of a range of potential solutions has often been useful. [9]

A choice work framing helps people disentangle and consider key components, conflicts, choices, and trade-offs inherent in an issue in ways that are accessible to a diverse audience. Presenting a range of perspectives and trade-offs, moreover, communicates that there is no simple right-or-wrong answer, but rather many possibilities that deserve consideration. It puts people in an active, problem-solving mode by signaling that they have been convened to consider alternatives and make headway on an issue, not to judge or be sold on a prepackaged set of answers by experts. Finally, the framework is moderator friendly and thus serves Public Agenda's goal of strengthening the capacity of a community to become more adept at dialogue and problem solving across boundaries.

Recruiting Participants. While Public Agenda provides guidance and support, it is the planning team that does the heavy lifting of recruiting citizens to the Community Conversations. The goal at this stage is to ensure that the conversation includes a truly inclusive cross section of the community. The aim is to reach beyond the usual suspects, with special attention to stakeholders with special knowledge or involvement with the issue at hand, the "unorganized" or general public, and traditionally marginalized groups.

There are, of course, very good reasons why some deliberative democratic methods recruit random samples of the public, and we certainly employ this formal approach to sampling in our qualitative and quantitative research. But in our Community Conversation work, we apply a "stakeholder" approach to participant recruitment for the following three reasons.[10]

First, during the original research and development on our Community Conversation model in the 1990s, we found that the best dialogue seemed to occur—both in our eyes and according to participants themselves in post-forum surveys—in discussion groups that were highly diverse. By this we mean not just demographic diversity (which is certainly important and which a random sample would tend to provide), but diversity in terms of participants' kinds of experience with the issue at hand. A stakeholder approach, with careful outreach and recruitment of participants who are directly affected by the issue, albeit in different ways, has a better chance of resulting in the type of diversity we look for. For instance, in dialogue groups on education, it was extremely useful to include parents, students, recent graduates, nonparent "taxpayers," employers, educators (from both K–12 and higher education), and others with varied stakes in and knowledge of student success. This kind of stakeholder diversity seems to elicit a great deal of social learning and "working through." "I've heard about the inner-city schools on the news, but this is the first time I've heard about it from a teacher who works in one, and it was a real eye-opener" is a characteristic statement we have heard in our debriefing interviews.

Second, while a random sample will tend to include members of traditionally disempowered groups, there are sometimes reasons to make sure these groups are particularly well represented. For instance, if the topic under consideration is immigration, it may be more important, from a community problem-solving perspective, to make sure that every discussion group includes immigrants than it is to ensure that their proportion in the overall forum matches their proportion in the larger population. The same principle holds for students and teachers when the topic is school reform.

Finally, follow-up action tends to be enhanced when a Community Conversation includes carefully targeted, diverse stakeholder groups. We've seen many examples of this, such as employers and teachers agreeing to get in touch about a class visit to a workplace that would show students real-world applications of their curriculum, or citizens deciding to volunteer for a community organization they learned about through another forum participant.[11]

Facilitating Dialogue in Small, Diverse Groups with Well-Trained, Local Moderators and Recorders. Large halls with hundreds of people elicit speech making, not the honest give-and-take and self-reflection of quality dialogue. Dialogue requires a small group, and that's where the real Community Conversation takes place. The typical Community Conversation involves roughly between 100 and 120 participants (although they have ranged from 40 to over 200), and often follows an evening schedule that begins with a meal and welcoming remarks. This is followed by two hours of discussion in diverse groups of 10 to 15 participants facilitated by local moderators and recorders trained by Public Agenda. A Choicework Discussion Starter (always in print form and sometimes in video) is used to launch the dialogue.

The small-group format is carefully structured, and local facilitators are trained to summarize their conversations using the following categories:

- areas of common ground (a platform for common action)
- areas of concern and disagreement (where more dialogue may be needed)
- questions or issues raised by the discussion (including information people need to move ahead in their thinking and actions)
- ideas for action and collaboration (less a specific action plan than a prioritized set of ideas and strategies that most agree ought to be seriously explored)
- next steps (by individual participants and dialogue organizers)

The forum closes with a short plenary session of small-group reports and final remarks, which set the stage for follow-up work.

What's Next? Moving from Deliberation to Action

From the start of the planning process, planning teams are coached to think about effective follow-up to their forums. At the very least, they are advised to provide a summary report to all participants, and to report results to decision makers and the local media. Whenever possible, they convey responses from decision makers back to participants. They are also encouraged to leverage the results in other ways to drive community change. For instance, they can create opportunities for inspired participants to roll up their sleeves and work on concrete actions through existing organizations, new task forces, or some form of political action.[12]

It's worth noting here that practitioners have a variety of views about how community dialogue and action ought to intersect. Some believe that community dialogue should avoid a focus on concrete problem solving and decision making, out of concern that such an emphasis will turn the Community Conversation into a high-stakes event that makes the honest exchange of ideas and insights difficult. Instead, from this perspective, the aim of community dialogue should be to build mutual understanding and relationships. More action-oriented and pragmatic community activists, on the other hand, tend to feel that words without action are meaningless, and they view a successful meeting as one that produces a detailed action plan.

At Public Agenda we adopt neither position as a rule and instead take a flexible approach, beginning by listening to the goals of the local organizers of a Community Conversation and then advising on how those goals might be achieved. To us, community dialogue and deliberation are best used to promote mutual understanding of a problem and develop directions that people are interested in exploring for solutions, but detailed action planning, we believe, is best handled in a follow-up stage by a variety of actors.

A Community Conversation can do a great deal to identify the ways in which policy and other forms of community problem solving can fruitfully move forward, and it can create momentum and legitimacy for change. But aiming for detailed action planning during a Community Conversation, which is the first time many participants have ever talked to one another, is often an unrealistic and distorting burden on the proceedings.

What Does Success Look Like?

Rather than calculating success by any one measure, such as policy change, we look for progress in many forms and by any combination of community actors, such as elected officials, civil society or business organizations, and ordinary citizens. Thus, while policy change is certainly one outcome that can occur, new partnerships, organizations, volunteers, behaviors, and attitudes can also be significant ways in which a community makes progress on a problem, whether it is workforce development or a public health concern.

Viewed in this light, a Community Conversation or other deliberative process should be positioned so it cannot be held hostage to the vagaries of any single actor's willingness to follow through. Because we recognize that it is difficult for citizens to make time to be involved in public life, we owe it to them to build in many different ways for their involvement to make a difference in the lives of their communities. Relying solely on policy makers for all follow-up action makes it more likely that nothing will happen and that citizens will feel their time was wasted. Therefore, we view the purpose of this work to be to enable many people and organizations to collaborate on a common problem. Success can thus come in many forms, as different actors learn from and leverage the Community Conversation process in different ways.

A second way we measure success is by the increased capacity for public engagement and collaborative problem solving over time, beyond any practical actions on the problem at hand. Such capacity building is about much more than simply learning how to execute a particular public forum model, as useful as that may be. It's about learning a set of flexible civic skills, strategies, and principles that are broadly applicable whether or not they are being employed in a formal public forum.

Authentic public engagement work requires that a coalition of community leaders grapple with a great many core elements of deliberative democratic work. These include coalition building, broad inclusivity, deliberative issue framing, sound processes of dialogue and its facilitation, and post-deliberation action. The experience of organizing, hosting, and capitalizing on a Community Conversation teaches a community about these principles and skills in ways that draw on their own unique assets and address their own unique challenges. In the process, this kind of work can change a community's leadership culture in several ways.

First, because meaningful community engagement is not about interest group politics as usual but rather boundary-crossing problem solving, planning teams often include actors and organizations that have rarely or never worked together. Frequently, there are strange bedfellows among them, such as business and unions, elementary schools and scientific research centers, grassroots neighborhood groups and banks, church groups and tax reform groups. Through the shared work of convening citizens in new ways, relationships form that can lead to collaborative activity down the road. Thus, viewing coalition building as integral to effective engagement helps community actors improve their capacity to communicate outside traditional silos and to identify shared interests.

Second, carefully designed community engagement efforts can profoundly transform the attitude leaders have toward the public and its democratic capacities. Public officials, for instance, can be excused for having a jaded attitude toward public forums, given how unpleasant they can be. (As one superintendent of schools put it, "I keep hearing about public engagement, but all I've experienced is public en*rage*ment.") It's no surprise, then, that public officials new to this work are often quite ambivalent about it, and it is particularly gratifying to see their reactions as they observe a Community Conversation. Often, they are happily shocked that a diverse group of citizens (sometimes including "troublemakers" who have harangued them at public hearings) can have productive conversations in which they listen and learn from one another.

Third, the experience can be powerful enough to change the way officials do business. A case in point was the aforementioned school superintendent, who went on to create an office of public engagement and institutionalize not only the Community Conversation as a yearly practice but also many other forms of community engagement, and has been continuing this effort for well over a decade. For many public officials, broad-based and inclusive public engagement practices have contributed to a culture of shared ownership of common problems that can help inoculate issues against hostile and pointless politicization. Simply put, when citizens and community leaders treat each other as allies in problem solving, they are more likely to behave as responsible partners instead of dissatisfied customers.

Finally, authentic and meaningful community engagement can lead to the emergence of new citizen leaders. Based on our observations and post-Conversation surveys over the years, the vast majority of participants in Community Conversations are significantly affected by the experience. They're more sensitized to the issue under discussion and talk about how they will act differently as a result. Often these are individual actions ("I'm going to talk to my son's teacher about that"; "I'm going to write to my representative"; "I will stop buying those products"). For other participants the impacts go further than personal attitude or behavioral change. These are the subset of Community Conversation participants who are willing to keep meeting with Community Conversation organizers to work on the issue under consideration in new ways.

It is not unusual, for instance, for a subset of participants and moderators to become so activated by the experience that they join the organizing team or some newly formed task force, or replicate the Community Conversation process in a new setting or for a new purpose. Strategies that are relatively simple and inexpensive make it more possible for community members to replicate or improvise on them once they have learned how they work. Their core components are thus more easily transferable to communities than complex and expensive methods, more easily "embedded" in the local culture of problem solving, and more likely, ultimately, to catalyze the energies of citizens and support what we call *deliberative efficacy*.

Traditional political efficacy is aimed at capturing the conditions under which individuals feel that they are capable of understanding political issues (internal efficacy), that their views matter to leaders, and that their vote counts (external efficacy). *Deliberative efficacy* is aimed at understanding the conditions under which individuals feel they are equipped to deliberate about problems and solutions; feel it is worth their time to be involved in collaborative problem-solving initiatives, such as deliberative forums; and feel that doing so is worthwhile because it can actually make a difference in the quality of life in their communities or in their own sense of connection to something vital outside their private sphere. Just as civil society actors and public officials can learn critical democratic skills in the context of organizing a Community Conversation, the impact on ordinary citizens' sense of deliberative efficacy is a crucial building block for emergent forms of leadership.

In sum, community engagement initiatives should be simple enough to be transferable to local communities while also ambitious and different enough from business as usual to stretch and stimulate a community's civic leadership network and produce significant learning for leaders, civil society actors, and citizens. Because they tend to produce rewarding results, public engagement strategies are likely to be used again as vehicles to include the public's voice and create new opportunities for problem solving. And because we promote the Community Conversation as a useful tool rather than a rigid formula, communities can and do improvise on the design once they have absorbed the core principles. A good illustration of how this looks in practice can be found in the case of Bridgeport, Connecticut.

The Case of Bridgeport, Connecticut: Embedding Patterns of Public Engagement

Formally launched in 1997, the Connecticut Community Conversations Project was a joint effort on the part of the Connecticut-based William Caspar Graustein Memorial Fund, Public Agenda, the Institute for Educational Leadership (IEL), and the Connecticut League of Women Voters.[13] Adopting the Community Conversation model originally designed and developed through the Public Agenda/IEL national project, the Connecticut Community Conversations Project has since spread to over a hundred towns and cities across the state.[14] Thousands of parents, education professionals, students, local policy and business leaders, seniors, and others have taken part in public dialogue on closing achievement gaps, ensuring school safety, promoting school readiness, preventing bullying, and many other youth-and-education topics.

While there have been many impressive results from this project, Bridgeport has distinguished itself in terms of the quantity of Community Conversations (well over forty so far) and in how the very fabric of public decision making has changed as a result. The Bridgeport Education Fund (BPEF), an organization dedicated to securing a quality public education for all children, has been a main catalyst for public deliberation in this region. The group's executive director, Margaret Hiller, is a prime example of what Harvard researchers Elena Fagotto and Archon Fung call a "deliberative entrepreneur," someone who imports and markets deliberative practices within their community.[15]

Since the mid-1990s, the BPEF has facilitated more than twenty-five Community Conversations itself and has helped other community organizations convene many more. In fact, Fagotto and Fung point out in their study that so many Bridgeport-based groups and organizations have used and adapted the Community Conversation model, it is difficult to determine the true scale of all the engagement activity that has taken place.[16]

Today, the BPEF is more than just a convener of community deliberations on education issues. It has become a dialogue-and-deliberation resource for other community groups working on a variety of issues, offering advice and training to organizers and moderators, helping groups frame issues for deliberation, and so on. Thus, what started as an experiment by one organization has blossomed into a new set of community practices and, in our opinion, a changed political culture.

Fostering "Thick" Public Engagement

Public engagement in Bridgeport was initially applied to problems in education and school reform. Over time, its use has broadened to neighboring issues, encompassing more and more aspects of public life. Engagement in Bridgeport has thus evolved from a relatively narrow stream of activity to an increasingly multilayered, "thick" community phenomenon. By this we mean it is no longer the province of one or two organizations focused on one or two issues, but rather it involves many kinds of community actors concerned about an array of issues.

The tracks of this migration, from narrowly focused to thick engagement, show how one issue—in this case, school reform—will reveal itself to be interconnected with many other community challenges. It shows as well how a social experiment can become a widely shared and transformative community practice. Public conversations in Bridgeport have now explored pre-kindergarten education for children suffering from mental health problems, after-school programming, achievement gaps, school safety, family violence, employment needs, corruption in city government, housing, economic development, and more. By the same token, numerous groups besides BPEF have taken part in a Community Conversation planning coalition, including the City of Bridgeport, the Board of Education, the United Way, the Regional Youth Adult Substance Abuse Project (RYASAP), the Bridgeport Child Advocacy Coalition, and the Bridgeport Regional Business Council. As BPEF director Marge Hiller explains this evolution, "The language becomes everybody's language. Everybody knows what a Community Conversation is. They know what engagement means. They also [understand that] this is how we have to make decisions."

From Thick Engagement to Significant Results

As Fagotto and Fung argue, "deliberative practices will yield more sustained effects when they are incorporated into—and thus when they transform—the communicative and decision making routines of organizations, institutions, and the communities of which they are part."[17] They refer to this process as "embeddedness" and identify three hallmarks of embedded deliberation: "a) the adaptation of deliberative models to address local issues; b) the adoption of public deliberation to advance the objectives of organizations or public institutions; and c) repeated use of public deliberation over time."[18] In the case of Bridgeport, it is clear that public engagement has become embedded, but the question of results remains: if public engagement is truly an important political practice, there ought to be something to show for it after more than ten years of application in a single community.

While causal connections are always difficult to trace in complex social systems, our interviews and observations suggest that important results have indeed begun to emerge, four of which we discuss in the following sections.

A More Engaged and Collaborative Political Culture

In our case study research in Bridgeport, many local leaders pointed to the way the political culture had been transformed as public engagement has become rooted in the life of the community. For example:

> When an organization or group thinks they want to find out about something, or come up with a plan, they automatically go to a large,

> broad-based practice, rather than saying, "Let's get the five or six best experts on this issue into a room to figure it out." —Adrianne Houel, Action for Bridgeport Community Development, Inc. (ABCD)[19]

> The development of community engagement as a standard operating procedure is, I would say, the most direct outcome of this work. The fact that it continues to be the way that things are done [in Bridgeport] is itself a real impact on relations and organizations. —Marge Hiller, Executive Director, BPEF

Local leaders also describe an unusual level of collaboration among organizations and service providers in the community, in large part because they now share a language and set of practices concerning effective community engagement. As one community leader told us, "We've got a much better tendency here to share leadership on things." A business leader added:

> What happened with the Community Conversation is there were some people that got involved from very, very different backgrounds. They worked really well together. They were willing to really share and collaborate. —Kathy Saint, President, Schwerdtle Stamp Company

As Fagotto and Fung note in their case study of the Connecticut Community Conversations Project, of which Bridgeport is a part:

> The Community Conversations are designed to promote coordination even prior to the deliberations. . . . The planning phase requires such a significant investment in terms of time and energy that conveners have an interest in maximizing the outcomes of conversations. Therefore organizers plan on how to use conversations' feedback to further their objectives.[20]

A More Active, Responsible Citizenry
with a Greater Capacity for Public Judgment

As this book argues throughout, sound, deliberative public engagement helps citizens develop a more realistic understanding of the trade-offs involved in difficult public problems and develop a sense of judgment. Based on what we've seen in Bridgeport, one of the byproducts of this development is an ability to hold leaders accountable in reasonable ways. As one community leader pointed out:

Issues can be complicated, and the more [ordinary citizens] are involved, the more they learn. That's very good. It creates a . . . raised base of knowledge in our community, and it means that there's more ability for parents and community members to assess what's happening and what should be happening, and to hold folks accountable. —Robert Francis, Executive Director, RYASAP

But if holding leaders accountable is one part of the equation, an equally important part is people's willingness to hold themselves accountable and share responsibility for solving problems. Francis continues:

We've had three or four years of strengthening our after-school programs. . . . It started very much as a community process with mostly just resident citizen types and young people and expanded. —Robert Francis, Executive Director, RYASAP

As these comments suggest, Bridgeport's culture of engagement appears to be contributing to the emergence of citizen leaders and an ethos of collective responsibility. As Fagotto and Fung note, these Community Conversations, "given the size of participants (around 100) and the focus on diversity, are an important tool to provide *community input* that can be used to create momentum, and promote action and policy change."[21]

More Inclusive Leadership and More Sustainable Policy

Just as it has changed the way average citizens look at community problems, public engagement has changed the way leaders look at citizens. In most communities, leaders engage with citizens as much, or more typically, as little as they wish. In Bridgeport, by contrast, business, education, and other community leaders told us repeatedly that they simply *must* consult with the community on important issues. As a result, leaders have been forced to slow down and be much more inclusive than they had previously been. In truth, they sometimes find this a frustrating process. But many also recognize that they are likely to produce more effective, longer-lasting solutions than if decisions were made by a few power wielders in isolation from the rest of the community. One community leader we spoke with noted how reassuring it can be in the policy process when "you know this is something the community believes in, this is something that the community has bought into, and this is something that they're willing to support."[22]

More Benefits for Kids

Over the course of our interviews with local leaders involved in the Community Conversations, we heard of numerous programs aimed at helping students thrive that stemmed substantially from the engagement work. Here is a sample of these activities:

- Eight hundred individuals volunteered to go to the public schools and read to children the day after a major education summit.
- Fifty-one mentors from area colleges worked one-on-one with two hundred high school students.
- School leadership teams (which had been established several years earlier and then abandoned) were reinstituted, giving parents a voice in school and after-school education policies.
- An anti-bullying policy was adopted and class size was lowered by the school system.

Another example shows how the public, under good deliberative conditions, can resist the temptation for wishful thinking and make tough choices. It involves a series of Community Conversations run by the Lighthouse After-School Program that uncovered a general consensus that, given the reality of limited resources, after-school activities should be focused on K–8 students instead of high school students. Lighthouse's leadership was surprised by this result, considering the level of concern about violence among older teens, but they took it seriously. When the time came to make difficult decisions about which programs to cut, they gave priority to protecting and expanding the K–8 programs. According to Lighthouse's director, Tammy Papa, there are now twenty expanded K–8 after-school programs throughout the city.

But while these programs may have done many kids a great deal of good, have they actually improved academic achievement in Bridgeport? Much remains to be done before anyone can claim that all children are being educated to their potential in that community. Still, there is significant evidence that this work has had a positive impact on student success:

- In the year and a half following a major education summit, over 90 percent of kids matched with a mentor showed improved school attendance and higher grades in math and social studies.
- Five Bridgeport schools have recently been removed from the list of poorly performing schools as a result of increased student achievement.

- The City of Bridgeport was one of five finalists in both 2006 and 2007 for the Broad Foundation Prize for Urban Education. This prestigious national prize honors urban school districts that demonstrate the greatest overall performance and improvement in student achievement while reducing achievement gaps among ethnic groups and between high- and low-income students.

In addition to the specific initiatives we've highlighted, another factor may be at work in promoting these results. Harvard professor Robert Putnam has found that the presence of high levels of "social capital" (norms and networks of trust and reciprocity) correlates powerfully with high school graduation rates, SAT scores, and other indicators of educational success. "States where citizens meet, join, vote, and trust in unusual measure boast consistently higher educational performance than states where citizens are less engaged with civic and community life," Putnam observes. His analysis finds that such engagement is "by far" a bigger indicator of educational outcomes than spending on education, teachers' salaries, class size, or students' socioeconomic status.[23]

Putnam's research suggests that some of the progress Bridgeport is making with respect to student success may not only be attributable to specific student success initiatives that have emerged through Community Conversations. It may also be an outcome of the social capital that this work generates and that might be creating a multitude of small, cumulative impacts through what people expect and how they think, act, and relate to one another and the community's children.

Public Agenda Today: Issues and Methods for a New Century

Tackling Twenty-First-Century Challenges: The Case of the Kansas City Math and Science Initiative

In 2006, the Ewing Marion Kauffman Foundation was just embarking on an initiative to improve science, technology, engineering, and math (STEM) education in the Kansas City region when it learned of Public Agenda's nationwide "Reality Check" research indicating satisfaction from parents and students with the STEM education in public schools. The Kauffman Foundation realized it couldn't just *tell* parents and students about the wonders of STEM subjects; instead, it sought to develop a serious and thorough *dialogue* within the entire community on the subject.

Public Agenda's work in Kansas City began with public opinion research aimed at learning how parents and students view STEM careers, the importance of these subjects in their lives, and the value they place on these fields of study in their school curriculum. The findings, based on focus groups, expert interviews, and a telephone survey of area parents and students, are summarized in the report "Important, but Not for Me."[24] The study added depth and local detail to the original "Reality Check" national study, but confirmed its basic theme: it was clear that Kansas and Missouri parents and students had not thought much about the importance of STEM education to twenty-first-century career opportunities, despite the importance that leaders and employers place on these subjects. But they were open to these ideas and had plenty to say about what would compel students to take more STEM classes.

The media and leadership attention to the study's release set the stage for the engagement work that followed. An accompanying memo to the report, "Engaging Stakeholders in the Kansas City Region on Improving Math, Science, and Technology Education," culled the research's strategic lessons for the engagement phase.[25] Finally, during this R&D phase Public Agenda created a *Community Conversation Toolkit* for improving STEM achievement, with a Choicework Discussion Starter video; a detailed manual for organizing Community Conversations; guides for participants, moderators, and recorders; and other tools and materials.

Building on the R&D phase, Public Agenda launched a three-year engagement program in the Greater Kansas City region (encompassing five counties in Kansas and Missouri) with the following goals:

- to help parents, students, and community members better understand the importance of STEM education
- to stimulate and inform action by educators, employers, families, and community leaders to improve STEM education
- to remove obstacles to collaboration across organizations concerned about STEM achievement
- to strengthen capacity for ongoing engagement beyond the span of the project

Public Agenda began its work by inviting local leaders to form a regional coalition to provide strategic guidance to the initiative and four interrelated strands of work: communicating opportunity, Community Conversations, leadership engagement, and online support.

With respect to communications, our research had pinpointed the importance of helping parents, students, and communities understand the opportunities connected to strong STEM skills. Part of our initiative, therefore, focuses on advising our partner communities on strategies to help close the "urgency gap" between the public on the one hand and leaders and employers on the other. As parents and students realize the direct connection between higher-level STEM and career prospects, they become more willing to engage in efforts to prepare students for success after high school.

On the Community Conversation track, hosting communities across the region were selected through an application process, after which local, nonpartisan planning teams were established. Public Agenda has supported these local leadership teams through planning workshops, facilitator trainings, small stipends, online collaboration platforms, and the tools and materials created for the initiative.

Coordination among the many organizations and entities that could have an impact on student success in STEM subjects—such as schools, employers, community-based organizations (CBOs), and preexisting STEM and workforce programs—turned out to be a vital need not being addressed by any single organization. The result has been inefficiency and duplication of efforts. Public Agenda was well positioned as an honest broker to facilitate dialogue and cooperation among long-standing entities working to improve STEM education, each in its own silo.

Our ability to serve in this role stems from two main factors. First, nonpartisan research is an important source of legitimacy, and the early research phase of our project, during which we interviewed local leaders and learned about the starting point of both the public and leaders, helped establish our credibility as the engagement phase of the project unfolded. Second, communities need neutral, honest brokers with no particular "dog in the hunt" other than general community progress. Through careful listening and ongoing relationship building, we were able to play a role in helping organizations pursue their own goals while helping create space for them to participate in larger community problem-solving processes.

The Kansas City initiative has also been a laboratory where we can experiment with ways of interweaving online strategies with face-to-face deliberation. Online platforms and tools have been useful, for instance, in helping community-based planning teams organize Community Conversations more efficiently to support post-forum planning for follow-up action. Online strategies have also helped us coordinate action among regional (not just community) leadership. Ultimately, we believe there is potential for regional leaders, in partnership with the growing number of individual communities organized around improving STEM education and school-workforce alignment, to use these online tools to disseminate innovations and coordinate

efforts, including potential joint policy initiatives. While many public problems are regional, most civic capacity-building efforts are local, and finding
a way to link the local to the regional level—especially in this complicated
two-state metro area context—is a challenge for which we believe online
strategies may be especially promising.

Using Web-Based and Multimedia Strategies
to Promote Public Judgment: Planet Forward and
the Public's Learning Curve on Energy and the Environment

The Kansas City case study shows how Public Agenda is increasingly inte-
grating online strategies into its community work. We've also been doing
much more in recent years to use the Internet and other media to engage
citizens and promote public judgment on a broader scale, beyond the community level.

Doing so builds on a longtime commitment to provide resources for
public deliberation through our website, which for over a decade has housed
deliberative guides that educators, students, journalists, and others have
used to better understand issues such as abortion, America's place in the
world, gay marriage, and the environment. A good recent example of a more
innovative approach to broad-based online and multimedia citizen engagement is the Planet Forward initiative, an innovative PBS pilot that combined opinion research, public engagement, and social media to create a citizen conversation on energy and the environment. Its unique design moved
from the web to television and back to the web, while using a citizen journalism strategy to spur citizen participation and create useful content.

Planet Forward was a production of the Public Affairs Project at George
Washington University and Nebraska Educational Telecommunications, in
collaboration with Public Agenda and Sunburst Creative Productions. Public Agenda contributed several key elements to the effort, beginning with
a major research initiative called the Energy Learning Curve. This survey
research was designed to produce more than just opinion data. It aimed to
provide leaders with practical insight into the public's readiness to engage
with a problem—in this case, energy. The Energy Learning Curve focused
on where public attitudes are firm and where they are weak, how much critical knowledge the public has, and whether people are prepared to make
trade-offs to achieve policy goals. In other words, it was designed very much
with Yankelovich's public judgment paradigm in mind.[26]

In addition, Public Agenda created the project's website (at *www.planet
forward.org*), which became a platform for receiving citizen input prior to

the television program in the form of videos, essays, poems, and songs on the theme "Can we get off fossil fuels? Should we?" There were more than a hundred contributors, from prominent figures like Microsoft cofounder Paul Allen, Maryland governor Martin O'Malley, and Stanford University scientists and engineers at the National Renewable Energy Laboratory to small business owners and students at George Washington University, Roger Williams University, and Middlebury College. The site posted contributions ranging from detailed statistical analyses to *South Park*–style cartoons. In addition to contributing ideas, site visitors could also shape the PBS program by voting for their favorite submissions.

An interesting cross section of contributions to the Planet Forward site was then included in the PBS television show. Hosted by veteran television journalist Frank Sesno, the program brought together citizens and policy makers in a unique format aimed at helping experts and citizens talk with each other rather than past each other—always a challenge for public engagement. Filmed in front of a studio audience and aired nationally on April 15, 2009, the program put citizen ideas in front of the nation's top thinkers on energy and allowed website contributors to share the stage with Carol Browner, President Obama's special adviser on climate change and energy. Other citizen videos and commentary from the website were discussed with several leading energy experts: Shai Agassi, founder and CEO of Better Place, a venture-backed company working to produce a market-based transportation infrastructure that supports electric vehicles; L. Hunter Lovins, president and founder of Natural Capitalism Solutions, which educates senior decision makers in business, government, and civil society to restore and enhance natural and human capital while increasing prosperity and quality of life; and James Connaughton, the former chair of the White House Council on Environmental Quality. In these ways, citizens and experts met on an equal footing for serious moderated discussion on a critical topic.

The special was carried by 96 percent of PBS stations and seen by 850,000 Americans during its first airing (figures comparable to those of other PBS public affairs shows and to cable news network programming in that time slot). It is noteworthy that the discussion among citizens and leaders didn't end with the airing of the show, as viewers were invited to submit new ideas for a web sequel, which aired on May 21 and featured President Obama's former Special Advisor for Green Jobs, Enterprise and Innovation at the White House Council on Environmental Quality, Van Jones.

The project demonstrated a unique strategy for employing the Internet and television to engage a large number of citizens, along with leaders, in an iterative and creative dialogue on a critical public issue. These sorts of experiments will be critical if the Internet is to become not just a means to network the like-minded in powerful ways, but an engine for democratic dialogue and problem solving among people with different values and starting points.

Helping to Build a Field and Movement: The Center for Advances in Public Engagement (CAPE)

The Kansas City Initiative is an example of how Public Agenda is attempting to strengthen the impacts of its work by employing research, community and leadership engagement, and various forms of communications in an integrated fashion. As we learn and experiment, we are also trying to strengthen the larger deliberative democracy/civic engagement field. That commitment has been formalized through the establishment of the Center for Advances in Public Engagement (CAPE).

In recent years, the movement that falls under the broad heading of deliberative democracy (or civic or public engagement, or citizen-centered politics) has exploded, with academic researchers and a growing number of nonprofit organizations working toward better public participation. Knowledge in this burgeoning field is certainly growing, but much remains to be learned about the strengths and weaknesses of different methods and how they fit different circumstances and needs; how to transform time-limited engagement projects into deeply embedded community practices; and how to leverage public engagement to have the most beneficial impacts on communities and public policy. CAPE was launched in 2006 to help meet these needs and has produced an array of case studies, evaluation tools, and research reports.[27] Alongside the public opinion research that typically launches our engagement initiatives, CAPE is the wellspring of another layer of research that helps us reflect on and sharpen our practice and contribute to the larger field. It is our way to institutionalize our commitment to learning how to help citizens come to public judgment in politically meaningful ways and to sharing what we learn with other practitioners and researchers.

CAPE Research Case in Point: Framing Impacts on Citizen Deliberation

A good example of a CAPE initiative to deepen understanding of how the public comes to judgment is an effort to learn about the impact of different types of issue framing on the capacity of diverse groups of individuals to engage in productive dialogue about complex issues.

The research tests ideas presented in Will Friedman's CAPE publication "Reframing Framing," in which he distinguishes between typical issue-framing efforts (framing to persuade) and the practice of framing issues in deliberation-friendly ways. [28] More specifically, the research compares the debate-style, pro-con issue framing that is characteristic of many media presentations with the type of framing accomplished through Choicework discussion guides that seek to clarify a range of positions and trade-offs involved in any problem. It aims to challenge the mainstream preoccupation with issue framing as the domain of power politics (e.g., partisan and interest group competition for citizen allegiance through persuasive framing) by exploring whether and how a deliberative approach to issue framing might help people grapple with difficult public problems and participate more productively in collaborative problem solving.

We first tested our hypothesis in four focus groups in Englewood, New Jersey, in 2008 by presenting two framings of Social Security reform. [29] In two of the groups, a moderator (who was, in research terms, "naive"—i.e., not informed of our research interests or hypothesis) used written material that framed the issue for persuasion by presenting two debate-style arguments about Social Security reform in a manner consistent with many media presentations. In the other two groups, the same moderator used written material that framed the issue for deliberation by presenting it in a Choicework format, with three different approaches to the problem and several trade-offs identified for each approach.

In all four groups, the moderator encouraged participants to react to the material they read and have a conversation about it, but very little formal moderating occurred. Rather than carefully guiding the discussion, the moderator asked participants to go over the Choicework guide and then begin sharing reactions. Occasionally the moderator would ask participants to say more or clarify a point, but beyond these occasional questions the moderator offered very little guidance for the discussion. The researchers observed the focus groups from behind two-way mirrors and had transcripts as well as DVDs of the conversations in order to study the results.

Our observations to date, summarized in the following sections, both confirm and inform Yankelovich's contention that helping the public encounter the choices surrounding an issue in nonpartisan and accessible ways is centrally relevant to helping citizens come to judgment.

Observation 1: Analysis versus Ideology. We observed that participants in deliberatively framed groups tended to discuss specific ideas related to the topic, such as how the Social Security program operates, whereas participants in persuasively framed groups tended to speak in sweeping, ideological generalizations about the nature of personal responsibility or the relationship between big government and personal freedom. In the groups framed for deliberation, we often heard things like the following:

> When Social Security was created, people weren't expected to be kicking around and playing golf for another twenty-six years. . . . Things are different now and the system needs to be overhauled to reflect that.
> —Male, deliberative framing group

> If Social Security is part of a "three-legged stool," it seems like we need to be thinking about how each of those legs works and how much, you know, like, weight each can take. —Female, deliberative framing group

> Right now I'm a full-time student and I work part time. The government's paying for me to go to school. It's a wonderful thing, because I would never be able to do it right now if I didn't get the grant. If they're going to cut all that kind of stuff out in order to pay for Social Security, a lot of people like me aren't going to be able to have good jobs because we won't be able to get an education. This is the kind of thing we need to think about before we just start saying, 'Hey, cut all the programs!' —Female, deliberative framing group

In the persuasively framed groups, by contrast, participants were far more likely to talk in broad generalizations. These conversations were often more overtly ideological and less specifically focused on the issue at hand. For example:

> The thing that's great about America is nobody forces you to do anything.
> —Male, persuasive framing group

> When [I] think about Social Security, [I] think about this money that you get from the government. I think about welfare . . . like government handouts. —Male, persuasive framing group

> All I'm saying is that I think personal responsibility is important.
> —Female, persuasive framing group

Observation 2: Curiosity versus Venting. We observed that deliberative framing led to discussions in which participants expressed greater inquisitiveness about the source and nature of the problems surrounding Social Security than did participants in groups with persuasive framing, which were marked by considerably more venting about things like corporate greed and government corruption.

To be sure, participants in the deliberative groups expressed a good measure of distrust of leaders and concerns about government accountability. Yet they seemed more able to move past their cynicism to ask questions about the nature of the Social Security solvency problem and express greater curiosity about how the problem evolved. Thus, for example, it was more common in the deliberatively framed groups to hear such questions as these:

> Where did the problem with Social Security come from? I mean, is it just because there are more people retiring now . . . or is it because there was something wrong with how it was set up originally? —Male, deliberative framing group

> My question would be the social context in which the Social Security program was created, and then how that's different from now—social, financial, group mentality. My question would be what are the differences between then and now? —Female, deliberative framing group

> So, if we were to privatize [Social Security] . . . what kind of transition would there be to make this new system work for people who are at all different places, from being young workers to those getting ready to retire? How would it work? That's what I'd like to know more about. —Female, deliberative framing group

For their part, participants in the groups with the persuasively framed, debate-style materials tended to spend significantly more time venting about corruption and greed, with comments like these:

> It's all about mismanagement and these politicians that they look for their own pockets to put money in there somehow, some way. I don't know who's doing what to whom, but that's what's going on. —Female, persuasive framing group

> The government officials are just trying not to get caught stealing money, having sex with hookers, or getting caught on drugs and alcohol. Never mind attacking a real issue like this. That would be insane. —Male, persuasive framing group

It may seem odd to juxtapose inquisitiveness and venting as we do here, but we observed that when the conversation got bogged down in venting about corrupt and greedy leaders— which happened more often in the persuasively framed groups—it seemed to circumvent people's curiosity about the nature of the problem. In short, it seemed as though venting about malfeasance furnished a kind of explanatory framework that made it more difficult for participants to be curious or interested in exploring the causes and nature of the Social Security solvency problem. Or perhaps it simply gave people an excuse not to work very hard by letting them fall back on pat explanations.

Observation 3: Hard Choices versus Easy Answers. Participants in the deliberatively framed groups were more realistic and pragmatic about the difficult choices involved in addressing Social Security problems, while participants in the persuasively framed groups did not articulate a strong grasp of practical choices and trade-offs and tended to reach for easy answers.

For instance, members of the deliberatively framed groups made these comments:

> The reason that we need to [deal with this problem] is because we have finite resources. We can't spend as much money as we want in every program. It's (a) irresponsible, (b) impractical, and so we have to look at the whole picture of the budget and say, "Well, how are we spending money as a society, and how are we valuing responsibility, and how do we define ethics as society?" —Female, deliberative framing group

> Overall, let me just say that I think none of these choices [presented in the Choicework Discussion Guide] alone—I think they're all somewhat rigid. When it comes down to Social Security reform, everyone's going to have to give a little bit—both on the right and the left. There's no magic bullet. —Male, deliberative framing group

For their part, participants in the persuasively framed groups did not tend to express a strong grasp of practical choices and trade-offs involved in either solution presented in their discussion guide. Rather than acknowledging that tough choices were needed, they were more likely to jump to answers like the following, which sounded easy and obvious but appeared to have little substance:

> I think we should do both . . . just make sure that there's enough money there for people and also sort of make sure that people save for themselves

and have control over their own money, but also make sure that the government can take care of people who end up at retirement and can't take care of themselves. That's what I'd like to see happen. —Female, persuasive framing group

I actually think the solution is simple, it's just some people don't like it. —Male, persuasive framing group

I think we should combine the two choices. I mean, it seems pretty easy. Why can't we have the best of both worlds? —Female, persuasive framing group

Observation 4: Solution-Oriented Creativity versus Off-Track Circularity. In addition to their being more analytical, curious, and willing to confront tough choices, we observed that participants in the deliberatively framed groups tended to be more solution oriented than their counterparts in the persuasively framed groups. Participants in the deliberatively framed groups appeared to work harder, exploring different directions, ideas, and possibilities in more depth. These comments on personal retirement accounts and privatization of Social Security are illustrative:

I assume that you'd be able to have some choices on a retirement fund, since it's your own money that's going in there. . . . Maybe privatization would work if they could figure out a way to help people learn how to pick the right funds and make the right investment choices. —Male, deliberative framing group

I'd be curious to explore some sort of incremental changes. I think currently FICA taxes only apply until what, the first $96,000 a year that you make? I'd be curious to talk about raising the retirement age and maybe lowering benefits. I don't know. It's hard, but it seems like things need to happen on lots of fronts. —Male, deliberative framing group

In the persuasively framed groups, these sorts of solution-oriented, problem-solving exchanges were less common. Instead, these groups tended to skid across the surface of many topics, sometimes repeatedly. They were also more likely to veer off into unrelated or tangentially related subjects like immigration (with comments about illegal residents claiming benefits) and education (with long conversations about the need for financial education). These groups tended to cover the same ground again and again, with some participants stating and restating the immediate conclusion they had come to upon first reading the debate-style materials.

Here is just a small sample of virtually identical comments made by participants in the persuasively framed groups:

> I'm against privatizing Social Security. . . . I'm against it, it's as simple as that. —Male, persuasive framing group

> I don't trust Wall Street any more than I trust the government. . . . All those guys just looking to make money for themselves could care less about my little account. I don't think it would work, personally, but I don't trust the government to handle it either. —Female, persuasive framing group

> I'd rather have control of it than have the government have control of it. That's just how I feel about it. —Male, persuasive framing group

Practical Considerations for Productive Politics. One way to integrate our four observations into a single framework is to say that participants in the persuasively framed groups were more likely to express their positions in static terms and circular patterns, while those in the deliberatively framed groups were more dynamic and focused on problem solving. People in the persuasively framed groups tended to come to a conclusion early and then cover the same ground over and over, as if they had landed once and for all on a position and had less incentive to explore new ideas. The cynicism that was more prevalent in these groups also seemed to hamper people's willingness and ability to engage in creative problem solving and instead appeared to bolster their static positions.

In the deliberatively framed groups, in which people were provided with some background on the issue, stimulated with questions, and offered a range of possible approaches rather than a polarized argument, participants were more likely to view the issue as complex and multifaceted. While it is difficult to capture this in quotes, we also observed that the overall tone of the deliberatively framed groups was more collaborative insofar as people held themselves and interacted as though they were *working* on a problem together, rather than simply reacting to the material and expressing static individual opinions in the presence of others.

What are the implications of these observations for our politics?

Downgrade Debate. The purpose of debate is to win an argument through persuasion, and it is therefore premised on the assumption that there is a clear right answer that will be revealed through the force of the better argument. Because debate is fundamentally competitive, it is a combative mechanism of disseminating ideas and information and is therefore better suited to a spectator model of public life in which citizens stand on the sidelines and watch "experts" battle on an issue in an effort to win them over to their side.

It is easy to see how a consumer model of citizenship might thrive under these circumstances, but is it really best for our democracy to reduce citizens to spectators and consumers of prepackaged decisions? Is it not reasonable to expect that the soaring levels of dissatisfaction and disengagement that tend to characterize public life (even during heady political times like these) might be directly connected to this model of information distribution—a model that both underscores the public's exclusion from important public decision-making processes and confirms the widespread suspicion among citizens that they are always being manipulated by leaders and the media?

In a society as complex as ours, public deliberation might be viewed as a therapeutic alternative to the consumer/spectator model of politics that only seems to amplify people's sense of alienation from public life. While debates are entertaining to watch and can, in moderation, serve a useful purpose in the American political landscape by helping people differentiate their choices, deliberation operates on a very different set of principles about how people can and should be able to encounter and navigate complex political issues.

Our point is not that there is no place for debate in a healthy democracy—certainly there is. Our point is that competitive debate and persuasion dominate our political culture and need to be balanced by more deliberative forms of political discourse. Whereas debate is competitive and spectatorial, public deliberation is collaborative and focuses on solving shared problems. As such, it assumes that many people have many pieces of the answer, and it is therefore fundamentally about listening to understand different points of view and discovering new options for addressing a problem.

Upgrade Deliberation and Active, Engaged Citizenship. Having issues framed for deliberation rather than persuasion is important because many of the issues we face in our communities and in our nation are highly complex, with difficult trade-offs that can be hard to uncover, unpack, and get a handle on. This is where the principles of deliberation come in, by help-ing people consider a variety of solutions and approaches and then develop common ground around those approaches together. But it is important to understand that deliberation is not a goal; it is a strategy and tool for over-coming hostile, dead-end, partisan rhetoric, for ending deadlock, and for helping citizens become vital partners in public problem solving.

Because deliberation is a strategy and a tool, it isn't merely about *talk-ing*. In successful deliberation, people work to make sense of a problem *and* to come up with specific ideas and actions for moving ahead on solutions. Therefore, the work of public deliberation is a cornerstone of democracy be-cause it involves the critical skills of citizenship that allow people to make informed decisions about difficult problems and play a more active role in partnering with leaders to solve the problems we face as a nation.

Conclusion: Toward More Integrative Insights and Methods

Over the thirty-plus years since Yankelovich and Vance came to the ideas that were to become Public Agenda, the core insights and mission animat-ing the work have remained the same:

- There is such a thing as quality in public opinion, and citizens can, under favorable conditions, come to meaningful terms with complex issues.
- Traditional opinion research and policy leadership fail to adequately appreciate the realities of the public's learning curve, but they would produce more beneficial results if they did.
- New forms of research should be developed to better understand how the public comes to judgment, where the public is in that process at a given point in time on a given issue, and what measures can help citizens work through the obstacles that hinder their progress.
- New forms of citizen engagement should be developed to help citizens come to judgment on problems and engage with leaders on solutions.

That said, the organization has hardly remained static through the years. It has evolved, first, in response to dramatically changing times: the emergence of the Internet and the ubiquity of information and misinformation; the deepening skepticism toward authority, the rise of partisan media, and the demand for voice; the nation's changing demographics and the demand for inclusion; and so on. All these shifts have led us to adjust our strategies and methods or add new ones to our repertoire, from increased use of web-based approaches to the frequent creation of Spanish and other language versions of citizen deliberation materials.

Public Agenda has also evolved as a result of what we've learned from both successes and setbacks in our efforts to support public judgment and link it to public problem solving. Our practices have evolved in how we present research to inform policy debates, engage leaders, and open up opportunities for public deliberation and participation; how we frame issues to make them accessible and useful to citizens and relevant to their learning curve; how we help strengthen capacity among local leadership coalitions for public engagement and collaborative problem solving; how we help apply the principles and processes of deliberative problem solving within institutions as well as communities; and how we help communities and citizens think more realistically and effectively about impacts, action, and change. (Will Friedman takes up this last question more fully in Chapter 6.)

We'll end with a few words about where we see the organization headed, in the hope that this is useful to the larger deliberative democracy field. Essentially, we see our work continuing to evolve through the integration of various strands of activity with the aspiration of creating more powerful and comprehensive approaches. Several examples follow.

Integrating Complementary Research Methods

On the research front, Public Agenda has for many years combined random-sample quantitative methods (which allow for scientific rigor and strong claims for generalization) with qualitative methods (which allow for exploration of themes with a depth and texture that elude poll questions). That these methods are applied with an appreciation for the stages and process of public judgment allows us, we believe, to report not only what people currently think and feel about an issue, but also "where they are" on their learning curves, the obstacles they face, and what would help them continue to come to terms with issues and develop a sense of responsible judgment.

A next step is to explore the integration of these traditional research methods with others in order to paint a more comprehensive, useful, and compelling portrait of people's evolving views and learning curve, and to inform policy making and public engagement in more powerful ways. One of these methods is community-based action research that enlists citizens themselves in exploring current and emerging views in ways that are tightly tied to community needs and change initiatives. Another method might involve new approaches to the deliberative research practiced by Viewpoint

Learning and James Fishkin, which seeks to study the public's thinking during and after deliberation. Yet another is systematic, longitudinal case studies that, like action research, can shed light on how citizens develop their views and their relationship with leaders in the context of their lived realities.

Integrating Public Research and Public Engagement

Increasingly, we see the benefits of combining research and public engagement in our efforts to inform policy, strengthen communities, and empower citizens. Preliminary research not only informs policy right off the bat by providing a reading of how the public and various stakeholders view an issue, but it also offers essential insights for engagement work aimed at fostering public judgment and various kinds of problem solving. Evaluative research adds a continuous learning loop to the work (which we embody in our Center for Advances in Public Engagement), which allows us not only to improve our own methods but also to contribute what we learn to the larger body of researchers and practitioners.

Integrating Public and Leadership Engagement

Our experiences with both stakeholder opinion research and community work suggest that the principles of effective public engagement (e.g., listening first, engaging stakeholders early and often, helping people understand the likely consequences of different courses of action, creating multiple opportunities for people to learn about and work on issues, and so on) can be productively applied to policy development as well. We are currently experimenting with applying these principles to policy contexts. One strategy we're developing as a complement to the traditional policy-brief approach to linking research and policy involves the creation of unique deliberative opportunities for leaders that take into account the specific legislative cultures in which policy decisions are made.

Integrating Community Engagement and Community Organizing

The potential synergy between broad-based public deliberation efforts and traditional community organizing approaches to citizen participation and problem solving is something we are also exploring. From our perspective, the entire engagement enterprise is concerned about including more voices in more meaningful ways and leveling the playing field so that everyone can participate effectively in decision making and problem solving on issues they care about. This certainly overlaps with the general thrust of community organizing in important ways.

Community organizing strategies that focus on empowering disenfran-
chised communities can be a powerful means to address power asymmetries
in ways that broad-based engagement may not be able to accomplish on its
own. At the same time, we see public deliberation as itself a means of not
only helping groups organize themselves but also becoming linked to the
broader public by building understanding and common ground across long-
established social boundaries.

Integrating Face-to-Face and Online Engagement

Today, public engagement has to adapt to the rapidly changing communication practices in our society. Computers and mobile phones have become
widespread, each supporting a broad variety of interwoven communication
media. Meanwhile, the target groups we are trying to reach in our engagement work have developed different patterns of communication. This leaves
us with a growing need for civic engagement efforts that offer multiple
channels of participation in order to be inclusive.

Over the last decade, online engagement methods have evolved and
matured, yet case studies and academic research show that the web is not
replacing traditional ways of civic engagement but rather expanding the
set of tools in the toolbox. The interaction between these different channels of participation still needs to be refined and best practices identified as
new platforms and tools reach critical mass and the general public adapts to
them.

• • •

As these examples show, our changing society and circumstances call for
new strategies to help citizens grapple effectively with complex issues and to
help experts and leaders understand and partner with the public in problem
solving. Yankelovich's insights remain as significant today as they were when
Coming to Public Judgment was first published. But it is crucial that we set
our sights on the leading edge of this work and continually look for new opportunities to push forward and innovate on behalf of an inclusive, meaningful democratic process—one that more powerfully helps communities
and the nation address the challenging issues we face.

CHAPTER 5

Moving Beyond Polls and Focus Groups

STEVEN A. ROSELL AND HEIDI GANTWERK

The Importance of "Working Through"

In *Coming to Public Judgment* in 1991, Daniel Yankelovich showed how polls and focus groups can be seriously misleading when the public has not made up its mind. More importantly, he identified three stages that the public goes through as it learns, forms its opinions, and reaches judgment: consciousness raising, working through, and resolution.

The second stage, working through, is too often ignored or taken for granted. In part this is because the conventional model of "informing and educating the public" assumes that people move from Stage 1 directly to Stage 3—from being informed to reaching a judgment. This assumption also helps explain why polls can be misleading on issues where people have not made up their minds—when they are still "working through" and have not yet reached resolution. Polls often measure how informed people are about an issue (Stage 1), but they seldom examine how far people have gone in working through the issue (Stage 2). People can be informed about an issue or proposed course of action but not yet have worked through the consequences and reached resolution. Polls taken at this first stage can overestimate the firmness of the views they are measuring and mislead policy makers.

While there are many examples of this, a classic one is the health care reform initiative led by Hillary Clinton during President Bill Clinton's first term in office. Polls showed strong majority support at the outset (which emboldened the administration to move forward), but that support dropped to barely a third of the public in a few months. The initial polls had been measuring raw opinion, not considered judgment, and it was easy for opponents to raise public doubts and fears.

More broadly, *Coming to Public Judgment* and the work it has inspired are part of a deeper transformation in how we lead and govern our organizations and societies.[1] Signs of that transformation include the restructuring of corporate and public bureaucracies to be more effective in dealing with rapid change; shifting boundaries between different sectors of society and levels of government; growing demands for a voice on the part of the public and stakeholder groups, resulting in the need for decision makers to consider many more viewpoints and challenges to the legitimacy of many traditional institutions. To succeed in this more interconnected and rapidly changing world, leaders in all sectors are recognizing the need to develop approaches to leadership and governance that are more participatory and more learning based. Today we often take these approaches for granted, forgetting that not so long ago they were rare. Here are some examples of these newer approaches:

- increasing use of executive and staff retreats within organizations in all sectors
- proliferation of conferences and other forums designed to foster dialogue and networking across organizational and other boundaries
- increasing emphasis on team building
- programs to foster diversity and inclusion
- the use of the Internet as a medium for networking, learning, and sharing knowledge around the world
- growing reliance on alternative dispute resolution
- more attention being paid to issues of values
- increasing efforts in all sectors to engage stakeholders in dialogue

Viewpoint Learning, Inc., was established to develop and apply dialogue-based methods that leaders and others can use to facilitate the process of working through (Stage 2 of *Coming to Public Judgment*) and more generally to develop learning-based approaches to leadership and governance in which many more people can participate. All of Viewpoint Learning's techniques build on dialogue as a form of social learning and as the "language" of working through.[2]

What Is Dialogue?

Dialogue is one of those words that everyone uses, but not always to mean the same thing. Misconceptions about dialogue abound, so it is important first to be clear what dialogue is *not*. For example:

- Dialogue is *not* a way to talk an issue to death (though this can happen when people misuse dialogue or don't know when and how to move from dialogue to decision making or action).
- Dialogue is *not* consensus building. Dialogue provides a better understanding of others' viewpoints, but it does not necessarily create agreement. What it ensures is that any remaining disagreement is based on real differences, not on misunderstanding or mistrust.
- Dialogue is *not* a systematic way of making policy decisions. When used properly, dialogue *precedes* negotiation or decision making; dialogue creates the broader perspective and shared language, the mutual trust and understanding that make subsequent negotiation or decision making more productive.

So if dialogue is *not* these things, what is it? Perhaps the quickest way to understand dialogue is by comparing it to its opposite, debate. Table 5.1 illustrates some of the key differences.

The key point is that debate and dialogue are based on different assumptions and have different purposes. Both are valuable. Dialogue does not replace debate or decision making; it *precedes* them.

Dialogue is a step that is too often left out in our traditional approaches to governance, decision making, and public learning. These approaches tend to be relatively simple—issues arise, key interests advocate for their preferred solution, and a decision is made. This may work well enough when the issues and the possible responses are reasonably well understood, and when those involved share similar assumptions, language, background, and culture. But when, as is increasingly common today, the nature of both the issues and the possible responses is unclear, and when people with very different beliefs, values, or traditions must find common ground, an additional step is needed. That is where dialogue comes in (see Figures 5.1 and 5.2).

Dialogue is the step we can take, before decisions are made, to uncover assumptions, broaden perspectives, build trust, and find common ground.

Whenever we conduct dialogues—whether with the public, business or community leaders, employees, elected officials, or other stakeholders—we begin with a set of ground rules (Fig. 5.3). The rest of this chapter describes

Table 5.1. Dialogue: The Opposite of Debate

Debate/Advocacy	Dialogue
Assuming there is one right answer (and you have it)	Assuming that others have pieces of the answer
Combative: attempting to prove the other side wrong	Collaborative: attempting to find common understanding
About winning	About finding common ground
Listening to find flaws and make counterarguments	Listening to understand
Defending your assumptions	Bringing up your assumptions for inspection and discussion
Searching for weaknesses and flaws in the other position	Searching for strengths and value in the other position
Seeking an outcome that agrees with your position	Discovering new possibilities and opportunities

how we have applied dialogue-based methods to contribute both to more reliable opinion research and to more effective governance.

More Reliable Opinion Research (Moving Beyond Polls and Focus Groups)

We developed the Choice-Dialogue methodology, based on the *Coming to Public Judgment* model, to provide insight that polls and focus groups cannot provide and were never intended to provide. Choice-Dialogues provide a way to compress (into an eight-hour day) and track the working-through process, in which dialogue participants come to understand the pros and cons of various choices, struggle with the necessary trade-offs of each, and come to a considered judgment. These dialogues, when conducted with a representative sample, offer deeper insight into the public's learning curve and how best to lead such a learning process on a larger scale.

Choice-Dialogue methodology differs from polls and focus groups in its purpose, advance preparation, and depth of inquiry.

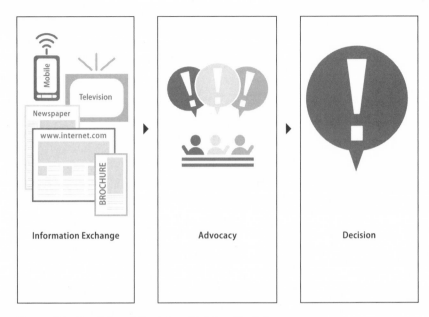

Figure 5.1. Traditional Decision-Making Models

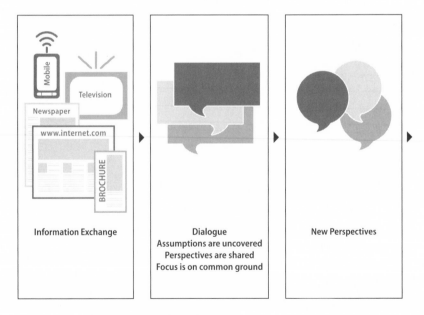

Figure 5.2. When Dialogue Occurs

The purpose of dialogue is to understand and learn from one another. You cannot "win" a dialogue.

1. Speak for yourself, not as a representative of a group or special interest.

2. Treat everyone in a dialogue as an equal: leave role, status, and stereotypes at the door.

3. Listen with empathy to the views of others.

4. Be open and listen to others even when you disagree; resist the temptation to rush to judgment.

5. Search for assumptions (especially your own).

6. Look for common ground.

7. Respect all points of view; all points of view will be recorded (without attribution).

Figure 5.3.
Ground Rules
for Dialogue

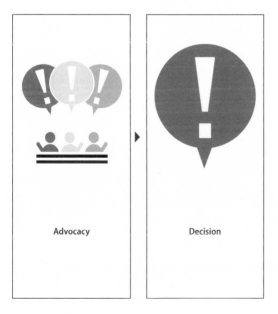

Advocacy   Decision

Purpose

While polls and focus groups provide an accurate snapshot of people's current thinking, Choice-Dialogues are designed to anticipate the future direction of people's views on important issues where they have not completely made up their minds, or when changed circumstances create new challenges that need to be recognized and addressed. Choice-Dialogues enable people to develop their own fully worked-through views on such issues (in dialogue with their peers) even if they have not previously given an issue much thought. By engaging representative samples of the population in this way, Choice-Dialogues provide unique insight into how people's views change as they learn, and can help identify areas of potential public support where leaders can successfully implement policies consonant with people's core values.

Advance Preparation

Choice-Dialogues require highly trained facilitators and the preparation of special workbooks that brief people on the issues. The workbook presents the issue, some basic background information, and (most important) a series of (two to four) values-based choices or scenarios for addressing the issue, written in the language of citizens (not experts). We have found that a format organized around values-based choices is critical because it enables people to absorb and apply complex information quickly. Each scenario consists of an introduction (a brief summary of what it is about), some basic background, a list of "key elements" (what steps would be taken to make this scenario happen), and a set of pros and cons (arguments for and against this scenario made by its supporters and opponents). The most important sections of the workbook (the ones on which participants spend the most time) are the pros and cons and the key elements. The advance preparation of these materials is a critical part of the Choice-Dialogue approach.

Depth of Inquiry

Unlike polls and focus groups, Choice-Dialogues are designed to explore how and why people's minds change as they learn. Choice-Dialogues are characterized by a huge amount of learning—participants learn both from the workbook and (more importantly) from one another. Choice-Dialogues are daylong, highly structured dialogues—twenty-four times as long as the average poll and four times as long as the average focus group. Typically, participants spend the morning familiarizing themselves with the scenarios and their pros and cons and developing (in dialogue with one another) their vision of the future they would like to see on the issue in question. They spend the afternoons testing their preferences against the hard and often painful trade-offs they would need to make to realize their vision. In this process people seldom simply choose one scenario, but instead mix and match to produce their own, revealing a lot about their underlying values and assumptions, the choices they would be willing to support, and the conditions for that support. To encourage learning, the Choice-Dialogue methodology is based on dialogue rather than debate; research and experience show that this is how public opinion really forms, by people talking with friends, neighbors, and coworkers. These eight-hour sessions allow intense social learning, and both quantitative and qualitative methods are used to determine how and why people's views change as they learn.

• • •

We have applied Choice-Dialogue methodology to a wide range of issues across North America, including health care, education, the federal deficit, entitlements, foreign policy, land use, housing, transportation, local budgeting, aging, and environmental sustainability. Two examples follow.

Citizen Values and the Future of Health Care in Canada

For many years the Canadian Health Care System has been the jewel in the crown and a fundamental element of the Canadian political identity: a first-rate, government-run health care program that provides top-level care to every Canadian.[3] But in recent years, the jewel has tarnished somewhat, and more and more Canadians have complained about rising costs, longer waits, and declining quality. Canada's federal government established a national commission to recommend reforms to address these concerns. Instead of relying solely on consultation with experts and representatives of special interests, the commission wanted to find a way to elicit and incorporate the views of "unorganized" citizens into their recommendations. But they recognized that polls and focus groups alone could not provide the insight they needed. While polls and focus groups clearly demonstrated that the public was dissatisfied with what it viewed as a serious decline in the quality of its health care system, these traditional research methods produced far less clarity about the sorts of solutions the public might be willing to support and the conditions that would make that support a reality.

The commission retained Viewpoint Learning to conduct a series of Choice-Dialogues across the country. In each daylong dialogue, a randomly selected representative sample of Canadians considered four very different values-based scenarios for health care reform. These choices ranged from significant tax increases to a shift toward a more market-based system in which people with more money could buy better coverage. All had significant support within "elite" circles. The dialogues showed Canadian policy makers that their latitude for action was broader than polls indicated. It also showed how resistant Canadians were to market-based solutions, in contrast to the American public. One proposal in particular, a major reorganization of primary care, had powerful benefits and appeals for Canadians (once they had a chance to work through the implications of this and other choices) that were not clear to policy makers beforehand.

The commission was able to use these insights into the public's core values on health care as "a compass" (as the staff director of the commission described it) to guide the reform proposals that were subsequently developed and are now being implemented.

Listening to Californians: Bridging the Disconnect

Viewpoint Learning, with support from the William and Flora Hewlett Foundation and the James Irvine Foundation, undertook a statewide Choice-Dialogue research project in California designed to provide state and local leaders with deeper insight into the views, values, and underlying assumptions of average Californians on some of the key issues and choices facing the state.[4] The purpose was to find practical ways to build the public support needed to effectively address important fiscal and policy challenges, and to improve the relationship between citizens and state and local government. Some dialogues considered issues from general policy areas (health care, K–12 education, and transportation), and some focused more on infrastructure (water, K–12 school facilities, and transportation).

What we found—in every dialogue, in every part of the state, and on every issue examined—was a profound mistrust of government and elected officials. This mistrust was both more intense and more persistent than expected, outstripping the levels measured by polls and focus groups. It emerged as a central underlying issue, shaping all other responses and undermining the ability to build essential public support on issue after issue. The research findings suggested a number of steps that leaders could take to break through this mistrust, build the public support needed to address important fiscal and policy challenges, and improve the relationship between citizens and state and local government.

Based on the interest in these findings expressed by leaders and others, three separate follow-up Choice-Dialogue studies were commissioned to examine three specific policy areas in greater depth: health care (sponsored by the California Endowment), K–12 education (sponsored by the

Hewlett Foundation), and the state budget process (sponsored by California Forward, a nonpartisan group promoting governance reform in California). Leaders from both parties played an active role in the design of these follow-up Choice-Dialogues. For example, on K–12 education we worked closely with representatives of the governor, speaker of the assembly, president pro tem of the state senate, and superintendent of public instruction. These dialogues provided more detail on the public's learning curve on each issue—how the public worked through the choices and trade-offs. They also detailed how the deep mistrust identified in the original study affected each issue and suggested "roadmaps" that leaders could use to build public support for reform in each area. The results were reviewed by leaders and other decision makers in Sacramento and across the state. *and what happened?*

More Effective Governance

Our initial goal was to develop the Choice-Dialogue methodology and apply it to a wide range of issues across North America. Having achieved this, our next step has been to look for better ways to combine research and application—to merge more reliable opinion research with more effective governance.

Our most recent work has aimed to extend the reach and the impact of this dialogue-based methodology in two directions. The first extends the dialogue to build ownership among key leaders (including groups traditionally focused on advocacy) and to experiment with ways of not just informing leaders but also engaging them in an ongoing two-way conversation. The second direction involves broadening the dialogue to include a larger cross section of the public. In other words, we have pursued two objectives:

- *Engaging leaders* early in the process to help frame and clarify the issue and to define the key choices and trade-offs. This approach is designed to ensure that the research is relevant to issues leaders face, to create a sense of authorship, and to increase the likelihood that the results will be heard and used. What we have found repeatedly is that the earlier leaders are involved in the process, the more likely it is that they will pay attention to the results.
- *Scaling up.* While the participants in the eight-hour Choice-Dialogues are deeply affected by the experience, developing the broad public understanding and support needed for significant policy reform

means casting a larger net—building on the insights of the research but using simpler and more targeted methods to engage many more people.

One current project provides a good example of how this approach works in practice and how these two objectives can be combined to reinforce each other.

Voices for Health Care: Advancing Sustainable Health Care Reform in Three States

Beginning in 2007, Viewpoint Learning, with support from the W. K. Kellogg Foundation, has worked in three states—Mississippi, Ohio, and Kansas—to engage both leaders and the public in a different kind of conversation to advance significant health care reform.[5]

The project's objectives include the following:

- identifying health care reforms to lower costs and improve access that both leaders and the public will support
- defining the roles of employers, the public sector, and individuals in such a system
- revealing potential roadblocks and conditions for support
- creating a roadmap that leaders and others can use to move these health care reforms forward
- developing a growing culture of and capacity for dialogue and civic engagement in each state where this work is conducted

In all these efforts, we have worked closely with local partners—state health care advocacy groups, which in turn brought in nonpartisan policy institutes as co-conveners.

The focus from the beginning has been to build momentum for significant change, with each activity leading naturally to the next. In each state the sequence was as follows:

1. Strategic Dialogues (one in each state), in which health care, political, civic, and business leaders worked together to create scenarios for reform to test with the public in Choice-Dialogues. Strategic Dialogue participants in each state arrived at surprisingly similar conclusions about the roots of the problem and the range of possible solutions that would be required to address it. Leaders participating in the Strategic Dialogues were impressed by the wide range of perspectives

at the table, the shared sense of urgency among people from different sectors, and the variety of expertise and experience represented. They appreciated the opportunity to move beyond short-term and incremental fixes to consider longer-term health care reform. Most were especially struck by the level of agreement about the need for significant reform and the core values all parties shared: they had not expected to find so much common ground on what could and should be done. Participants ended the day with a growing sense of what might be possible, curiosity about what the Choice-Dialogues would reveal, and interest in the project and its prospects. These sessions built a sense of ownership of the subsequent phases of the project and began to build momentum for broadening public engagement efforts.

2. Nine daylong Choice-Dialogues (three in each state) in which randomly selected, representative samples of the public explored what sort of health care system they wanted to see in the future, grappling with the difficult choices and trade-offs involved. As a starting point, participants used a special workbook constructed around four distinct scenarios for health care reform. These scenarios, based on leaders' conclusions in the Strategic Dialogues, were written in the language of citizens and designed to highlight the key values and trade-offs. These scenarios provided a *starting point only*—participants were free to change or combine them as they saw fit. The four scenarios were as follows:

   a. Shared responsibility (requiring employers, government, insurers, and providers to share responsibility for fixing the holes in the current employer-based insurance system)
   b. Increasing personal responsibility (requiring each state resident to have at least minimum health insurance coverage coupled with measures to make coverage more affordable and to increase public education about health)
   c. Public health insurance for all (creating a state agency to act as a single insurance company for all state residents)
   d. A coordinated wellness system (ensuring that every state resident has a "medical home" that provides coordinated care and emphasizes wellness and prevention)

In all nine Choice-Dialogues, across three states and a wide range of specific local circumstances, participants followed very similar steps and reached a strikingly consistent set of conclusions. At the outset, participants in all dialogues quickly agreed that the health care system has major problems and that something significant has to change. Stereotypes about the uninsured began to fall away as people with and without insurance talked directly with one another. As they compared experiences, they realized that the problems affected everyone in the room, insured and uninsured alike, and that in fact they were all paying for the uninsured already. In working it through, they concluded that everyone needed to be covered—but how? They first looked to the employer-based system, which was familiar and offered choice and competition. But they saw that fewer employers could afford coverage, that self-employed and part-time workers had no coverage, and that having to fund health care made companies less competitive. So they asked whether the state could do better.

Participants had major concerns about a state-run system—in particular, that it would restrict choice, cover "freeloaders," and cost too much. Over the course of the day they worked through each of these concerns in turn. For example, on choice, they agreed that any state system would have to allow choice of providers. But they also agreed that it was unrealistic to have unlimited coverage of treatments and concluded that a state-run system should cover only treatments that had been scientifically proven effective (evidence-based medicine), on condition that there was an appeal mechanism and access to second opinions. Participants also agreed that while the state should provide basic coverage to everyone, employers or individuals should be able to provide supplemental coverage. By the end of the day, strong majorities in all dialogues (including majorities of both liberals and conservatives) supported switching to a publicly run health system that would be paid for by taxes. They also agreed to a number of steps to improve wellness, emphasizing that we not only need to cover everyone but must have a system that makes people healthier. Even more striking, they agreed to pay more in taxes for such a system—on the condition that the funds were earmarked for health care and that there was strong accountability for how funds would be spent. Their basic conclusion was that we are already paying for a system that doesn't meet our needs; let's pay for one that does.

3. An Interactive Briefing with leaders, including many who had participated in the Strategic Dialogue as well as others from business, government, health care, and other sectors.[6] Leaders were surprised and encouraged by the amount of common ground identified by Choice-Dialogue participants, and also by their thoughtfulness and their willingness to confront difficult choices. In particular they

were surprised by citizens' openness to a public system, their strong support for preventive care, their support for electronic record keeping, and their broad-based willingness to pay for a system that provides everyone with access to care. The fact that such diverse groups had reached strong conclusions led even the skeptics to conclude that they had more leeway than they had previously thought to engage their constituencies, colleagues, and organizations in a tough-minded conversation about potential reform. The discussion in these sessions focused not only on the substance of the findings but also on ways to build on the results, reach out to other leaders, and continue to engage with the public.

The remaining elements of this project (currently under way) focus on "scaling up" the dialogue to engage a broader cross section of the public. These efforts encourage people to grapple with the difficult choices involved using a variety of structured face-to-face and online methods. Just as important, they allow leaders in each state to develop and deepen local institutional capacity for dialogue and public engagement—around health care as well as other challenges facing their state.

4. Based on the Choice-Dialogue findings, we developed a Meeting-in-a-Box kit that enables leaders, advocates, and others to conduct two-and-a-half-hour, highly structured community conversations about health care reform. The kit includes feedback mechanisms that can be used to measure results and build a list of interested citizens who can continue to engage with the issue over time. Our local partners recruited local facilitators whom we trained in the use of the Meeting-in-a-Box kit, and many community conversations are now under way in each state. Hundreds of people have already participated in Community Conversations. Our local partners also report a number of other tangible benefits: wider awareness of their organizations, increased visibility and credibility as a state leader on health reform, and a growing and more energized network of citizens interested and engaged in the discussion of health care reform.

5. On-Line Dialogue included participants from each of the target states and from across the country. It provided more citizens with an opportunity to engage in a dialogue on health care reform online and to contribute their views. This dialogue was widely promoted by state partners, as well as on the Internet and through Facebook. It included an online Choice-Book—a user-friendly way for individuals

to work through a simplified version of the Choice-Dialogue scenarios. As they worked through the Choice-Book, participants responded to each scenario and completed a brief questionnaire on their values and priorities; at the end of the Choice-Book phase, each participant received a customized report outlining how his or her responses compared to those of most participants. Participants then had the option to sign up for an online "small group dialogue" in which they worked in small, moderated groups to go deeper into the issues and trade-offs raised in the Choice-Book.

6.   In parallel with these efforts, we have conducted ongoing outreach through local communications and media activities to heighten public awareness of these efforts and create "buzz" around the need for reform and the specific approaches identified by the public and leaders.

how do you scale

Many leaders who observed the Choice-Dialogues and participated in the Strategic Dialogues and Interactive Briefings were surprised at what they saw. Participants (leaders and "regular" citizens alike) were engaged, passionate, and thoughtful about the choices they had to make, and they were willing to consider sacrifices and trade-offs to create a better system for everyone. Citizens who participated in the Choice-Dialogues were surprised as well; many said it was the first time they had ever been asked to weigh in on an important policy question, and they were eager to stay involved. They also expressed amazement at the level of civility and the power of dialogue to move past partisan division and toward mutual understanding. These sessions revealed a hunger for engagement and a demand for leadership among residents in each of the target states.

The *Voices for Health Care* project provides one promising example of how more reliable opinion research can be combined with efforts to more fully engage leaders and the public in improving governance.

Challenges and Next Steps

More than seventy-five years of experience with polls has demonstrated their enduring value as a cost-effective way of measuring the views of a large population through scientific sampling. This experience has also taught us some of the major limitations of polling—in particular that it can be misleading when the public has not made up its mind (often the case on complex policy issues). *Coming to Public Judgment* analyzed these limitations and also proposed a way to overcome them.

Our work at Viewpoint Learning, and the examples described in this chapter, are part of an effort to develop new methods of opinion research that do something different: methods whose strength is polls' weakness. These new methods help people make up their minds—accelerating the working-through process. They document the public's learning curve and provide a different kind of insight that can complement and sometimes correct the insight provided by polls and focus groups.

But the question remains: Why do polls and focus groups alone continue to be the methods of choice for hearing the voice of the unorganized public, and for gauging public views and values on all issues, long after *Coming to Public Judgment* showed their limitations? The answers that follow reveal some of the key challenges that lie ahead both for new forms of opinion research like Choice-Dialogues and for efforts to engage more people in governance (especially the unorganized or unaffiliated public).

Most Leaders Understand the Value of Polls but Not Their Limitations

We need to do a better job of familiarizing leaders with the limitations of polls (when people have not yet made up their minds), and especially with how newer, dialogue-based methods of research and engagement can help them govern more effectively. As our society becomes more fragmented and the number and range of interest groups grow, these new methods can help leaders to better hear and understand the voices of the unorganized public (reaching past interest groups), build public support (especially on gridlock issues), and find common ground. But the first step is to make leaders aware that there are tested alternatives to the traditional top-down model of "informing and educating" the public, and to the more limited insights that polls and focus groups alone can provide.

A Polling Story Is Easier to Tell Than a Dialogue or Deliberation Story

Fundamental changes in the media and the emergence of new media have contributed to a further fragmentation of the public. For example, it is becoming more common today for people to view only news sources that agree with their own viewpoint. This combined with a shortening of attention spans and a reduced attention to context makes working through and finding common ground even more difficult. We need to find better ways for the media, and especially new media, to tell a deliberation story and to contribute to "scaling up" this sort of dialogue.

One major challenge is that the mainstream media (especially radio and television) tend to focus on conflict and extreme views rather than on finding common ground. Recently, for example, some citizens who had participated in one of our dialogues were interviewed on a nationally syndicated radio program. The interviewer asked us to send an equal number of people who identified themselves as Republicans and Democrats, which was easy to do. During the interview he repeatedly tried to find areas of disagreement between these groups and was increasingly skeptical and frustrated when the citizens told him that they really did agree on the important questions and that any disagreements were secondary. All the participants, in their own way, tried to get across that the big story for them was precisely that there was not the expected division and that there was far more common ground than any of them had expected. It seemed to us that because the interviewer couldn't identify a conflict or wedge issue, he didn't know how to tell the story. Afterward, one participant remarked to us, "He didn't seem interested that we found common ground on anything. He just wanted us to argue and disagree. Why couldn't he understand that we got past all that stuff?" We are now working with media producers to experiment with ways in which using dialogue to find common ground can be "good television," but much work remains to be done.

Because These Dialogue-Based Methods Are Relatively New, They Cost More

Bringing down the cost of these better ways of listening to and engaging the unorganized public means enabling more people and organizations to learn these techniques and, over time, institutionalizing an ongoing public capacity for dialogue. We should not have to reinvent the wheel each time we want to bring the voice of the public into the governance process. It should be a regular part of our political culture and how we do public business.

Conclusions

Coming to Public Judgment provided critical insight into how the public learns and reaches judgment—that is, into the public's learning curve. That insight has been central to the efforts described in this chapter to develop more reliable methods of opinion research, to engage the public, and to strengthen governance and leadership.

There are a number of key lessons we have learned in this process that can help guide efforts to meet the challenges and take the steps described in the previous section.

The Value of Bringing Together Citizens with Very Different Backgrounds and Viewpoints

Too often today conversations about public issues take place only among groups of the like-minded. These narrower conversations tend to reinforce polarization of different groups, increase the stereotyping of "others"—those who hold different views and make different assumptions—and limit learning. In a dialogue, by contrast (and unlike a negotiation), the more diverse the perspectives of the participants, the richer the learning and the more productive the outcome. On issue after issue, we have found that when citizens are given an opportunity to look at the bigger picture, to connect the dots, and to engage in dialogue with others from very different backgrounds and perspectives, they think and act more like citizens and less like consumers, they develop a shared community perspective, and they are ready to make and support big changes to advance the common good.

The Power of Building on Common Ground

Over the years, the clash of interest groups has created or reinforced gridlock on a growing number of issues—education, immigration, health care, taxation, and budgets, to name just a few. *But it is important to realize that this is a gridlock of special interests, not a gridlock of the public.* We have repeatedly found, in our work across the country, that citizens who begin with very different viewpoints can find a remarkable amount of common ground. It is on such areas of common ground that effective leaders can build broad-based public support for action. Building on common ground is a way to increase trust and move toward sustainable solutions, while building on wedge issues tends to reinforce polarization and gridlock.

The Changing Expectations of the Public

In our work in the United States over the last couple of years, we have seen a change in Americans' expectations of their leaders and of themselves. This change comes in part from a growing sense of crisis about the direction of the country and (especially) the troubles of the economy—including a growing anxiety that we as a nation are living beyond our means and that leaders are disconnected from citizens' concerns. Much more than before, Americans are telling us the following:

- They want leaders to provide an honest, straightforward assessment of the challenges facing the nation. They are increasingly suspicious of easy answers and more aware when they are being pandered to or misled; such tactics tend to reinforce mistrust.

- They do not expect leaders to provide all the answers—but they do expect leaders to give people the chance to wrestle with the tough choices and to take citizens' viewpoints seriously.
- They want to be challenged and play a role in problem solving: being asked to consider hard choices is not a poison pill.

These expectations cut across the usual demographic and political categories.

Responding to these expectations will create a major challenge for elected officials at all levels of government. But it also provides opportunities for leaders and for everyone who has been inspired by *Coming to Public Judgment* to make the public's voice a foundation for governance and leadership.

PART III

EXPLORING NEXT STEPS

CHAPTER 6

Coming to Public Judgment

Strengthening Impacts,

Exploring National Possibilities

WILL FRIEDMAN

Coming to Public Judgment was no mere intellectual exercise. Dan Yankelovich wrote it in order to improve the quality of our democracy not only by showing that the public is *capable* of politically meaningful judgment but also by outlining ways to intentionally *bring it about* more effectively and efficiently as a means to inform and legitimize public policy.

The three applied chapters in the present volume—on the National Issues Forums; Viewpoint Learning's deliberative approach to research; and Public Agenda's varied efforts to both support and research public engagement—each demonstrate the ability of citizens to "work through" tough issues toward judgment. Together they amount to a compelling demonstration that the public can, under the right conditions and with the right tools, grapple effectively with even complex policy questions. What is less clear, and what represents the leading edge of "public judgment politics," is how to meet two challenges: ensuring that efforts to support public judgment lead to significant impacts; and scaling up deliberative work from the local level, where it has been applied most successfully, to the level of national politics.

These challenges are especially meaningful in the current political context of the Obama administration's exciting, yet ambivalent and somewhat confused, openness to a more engaged citizenry. The opportunities created by the Obama administration could, if carefully nurtured, lead to real breakthroughs. But if they are mishandled, they could end up as missed opportunities or even setbacks to the possibility for a more inclusive and deliberative American democracy.

Public Judgment and Social and Political Change

Yankelovich argues that the public's potential and appropriate role in the policy process is underappreciated by decision makers because of the cultural divide between them and ordinary citizens. Leaders rely on prominent experts who operate within the culture of technical expertise, the mode of knowing and doing that prevails in our elite political culture.[1] This prevents both leaders and experts from recognizing, let alone promoting or being guided by, the possibility of public judgment. The implication of this analysis is that if this cultural gap could be bridged by a pragmatic understanding of the nature and process of public judgment, leaders could begin to take the public's views into account much more effectively in formulating public policy.

And, indeed, there is evidence, some of which I'll discuss in a moment, that local leaders are beginning to better understand and increasingly act on the need to thoughtfully engage their publics in the policy process. That said, challenges that arise in practice suggest that an analysis focusing almost exclusively on the disconnect between leaders and the public leaves power relations and conflicts of interest too much out of the equation. For even if leaders and experts were to appreciate the difference between raw opinion and public judgment, the application of public judgment to our nation's problems could hardly be considered a foregone conclusion. Yankelovich acknowledges this point in passing when he writes:

> It would be an exaggeration to imply that if the public [works] through its ambivalent feelings on [controversial] issues, resolution would automatically follow. Having people make up their minds is a necessary condition to resolving most issues legally and politically, but it is rarely a sufficient condition. On some issues, strategically placed special interests thwart the public will. On others, resources may be lacking, or strong leadership, or a basis for compromise. Putting an end to public waffling may not be enough to insure political resolution, but it hastens the process radically. The matter can be stated simply: *without* public judgment, issues fester unresolved without time limit; *with* public judgment, issues can be resolved quickly, saving years of strife, turmoil, waste, and danger.[2]

My point is that in order for public judgment to matter in the real world, a great deal more attention must be paid to all the ways in which the public will can be thwarted by "special interests," "lack of resources," and "weak leadership," not to mention such hindrances as outright corruption.

This is not to say that interest group and advocacy politics per se thwart public judgment, but that excessive versions of them that are not balanced by less partisan modes of public engagement can do so. These factors have much more to do with power disparities than with the culture of expertise, and they are, of course, familiar features of traditional political analysis. Because they can obstruct the impacts that deliberative democrats intend, we need to learn more about how to talk about them, analyze them, and address them in the context of our work. We will be aided in doing so if we first articulate our understanding of how public judgment leads to various kinds of social and political change, which will then allow us to examine how and when power imbalances come into play as obstacles we must negotiate or otherwise confront.

In Chapter 1 of this volume, Yankelovich models the process of the public's learning curve toward judgment, as shown again in Figure 6.1.

We can build on this framework to envision a fuller model of deliberative democratic change by attempting to articulate more of what happens *after* the public comes to judgment, which, based on my reading of Yankelovich, would be something like the model in Figure 6.2.

That is, as citizens engage with issues and a sense of public judgment emerges, the public informs leadership action by identifying the sorts of policies that are aligned with people's values and their willingness to accept trade-offs. This evolution of public opinion also creates new societal norms that lead to broad-based cultural and societal shifts, as in the example that Yankelovich often cites of the history of women in the workplace over the past century or so.[3]

Building on this framework, we can add several elements that will more fully account for how deliberative politics leads to change, as well as where and when its practitioners must be prepared to address power issues. Such a model should encompass at least *two types of change* that this work can bring about as well as at least *three kinds of actors* who can effect these changes in communities and institutions.

The two types of change that deliberative work should aim for are (1) progress on concrete problems and (2) an increased capacity for democratic problem solving. That is, we want this work to help communities and the nation make real progress on real issues *and* we want it to instill a greater ability for effective, inclusive, deliberative problem solving.

In our article "Deliberative Democracy and the Problem of Power," Ali-

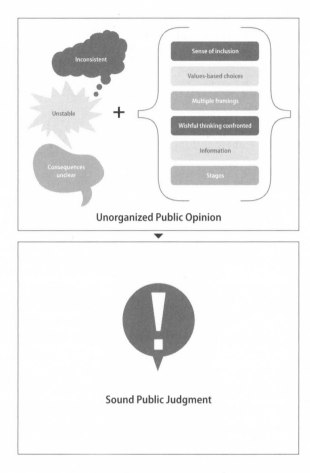

Figure 6.1

son Kadlec and I borrow John Dewey's term "social intelligence" to talk about the latter kind of change, by which we mean, essentially, people's capacity to address common problems in concert with others. We discuss the interrelation of these twin goals of engagement in the following terms:

> Social intelligence and concrete problem-solving are . . . two dimensions of the same process of deliberative democratic change. Citizens typically get drawn into processes of deliberative engagement because they want a real voice in addressing tangible problems facing their communities. Once so engaged they often find the experience of well-designed deliberation intrinsically satisfying and stimulating. At this point our two dimensions of change can become highly reinforcing in a kind of virtuous cycle:

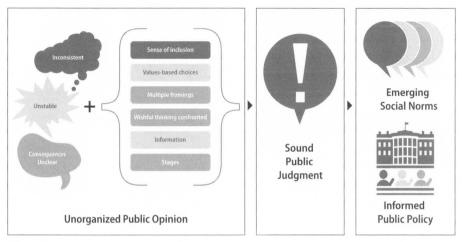

Figure 6.2

as an intrinsically stimulating democratic involvement that also helps address concrete public problems makes people want to *stay* engaged, their democratic capacities develop (they become better at it) . . . and the process becomes at once more satisfying, stimulating, effective and meaningful.[4]

A capacity-building orientation that seeks to "embed" deliberation rather than simply enacting it in a given deliberative event is particularly important from a public judgment perspective.[5] Yankelovich's discussion of "time-lag" problems in this volume highlights the fact that coming to public judgment requires iterative opportunities through which people learn more over time. Single deliberative events, while sometimes useful for particular purposes, will rarely be enough to help significant numbers of citizens work through knotty and multi-layered issues.[6]

Moving from ends to means, there are at least three sets of actors that can translate processes of public deliberation into the twin outcomes just enumerated: public officials; nongovernmental organizations and leaders (or NGOs, such as civil society organizations, grassroots community groups, and business associations); and citizens themselves (individually and in groups). Action by any one or all of these sorts of actors can begin to leverage processes of public deliberation and an emerging sense of public judgment in ways that solve problems and build democratic problem-solving capacity.

For instance, if the issue at hand is creating better after-school programming for a community's children, public deliberation can lead to a clarity about priorities and direction that can spur action by mayors, schools, the PTA, the Boys and Girls Club, parents, and youth leaders. This speaks to progress on a concrete problem, certainly. But it can also lead to new problem-solving capacity if, in the course of deciding and working on the issue, various community actors learn new skills, develop new relationships, and begin to establish new democratic norms and expectations.[7]

Figure 6.3 adds these ideas to the picture of public judgment and change that we began to construct earlier.

Confronting Power Imbalances in Order to Ensure Deliberative Democratic Impacts

This framework for understanding deliberative democratic change shines some light on the problem of power discussed at the beginning of this section, for it suggests that at least two points in the deliberative process when dealing with power imbalances will require special attention. One is at the stage of public engagement (lower left in Figure 6.3); the other is at the stage of action to make progress on concrete problems (lower right).

Public engagement practitioners must confront power issues and imbalances, first, at the stage at which they are attempting to create the conditions necessary for inclusive, productive, and legitimate participation. In one sense the very purpose of working to put public engagement processes into play is to compensate for inadequate or unequal opportunities to engage in public life. Much deliberative democratic work is therefore aimed at leveling the playing field so that more voices can be heard, more ideas can be considered, and more interests can be taken into account as problems are confronted and decisions are made that affect everyone's well-being.

The second place where power dynamics must be addressed is in the post-deliberation, post-judgment phase to help ensure that engagement leads to meaningful results. Because the levers of change tend to be most heavily influenced by those with the greatest resources, as in public policy development, deliberative democratic work should aim to ensure that decision makers take public engagement seriously and that other avenues of progress (such as grassroots action or better coordinated programs by civil society organizations) are pursued as well.

What it means exactly for public officials to "take seriously" the public's deliberations is, of course, no simple matter. It would not generally make sense, for instance, if leaders were obligated to perform every action that emerged from a given public deliberation process. That would be imprac-

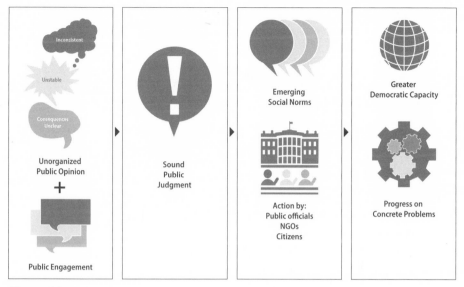

Figure 6.3

tical, overly rigid, and often highly problematic. But just as unsatisfying is the ability of leaders to cherry-pick from the results of public deliberation which ideas and priorities they will pay attention to and how seriously they will take them. This leaves too much room for conciliatory posturing to substitute for authentic responsiveness by officials and meaningful influence by citizens. Some middle ground needs to be established, along with a reasonable degree of accountability that makes sense in the context of a more deliberative politics and helps ensure that people's participation leads to meaningful outcomes.[8]

What might a deliberative democratic concept of political accountability look like? First, if leaders should not be expected to enact every idea that emerges from the public's deliberations, they should at least be expected to say why they choose to respond more to some and less to others. They should, in other words, be expected to continue the dialogue on issues so that citizens and leaders alike can continue on their respective learning curves.[9]

A deliberative democratic concept of political accountability would also place demands on other actors. As argued earlier, not only public officials but NGOs and citizens themselves are potential change agents that can help create a bridge from an emerging sense of public judgment to various forms of problem solving. That being the case, accountability, in some sense, falls on them as well to do their part to bring about needed change.

Once again, what this means in practice is no simple affair. People are exceedingly busy with all sorts of important matters (their families, for instance), and few will or should drop everything to work for a new cause. Community-based organizations likewise have their hands full doing good work already. Neither citizens nor organizations should be required or guilt-tripped into joining elaborate new activities that conform with some deliberative democrat's idealized notion of the active citizen and engaged community—nor, as a practical matter, can they be.

But often, it is more a matter of adjusting what one is already doing than of adding something arduous to one's agenda. Citizens may, as a result of public deliberation, speak differently to their children's teachers, question candidates more insightfully, or shift their volunteer efforts from one activity to another rather than join a newly created task force. Based on my experience in a great many communities supporting public deliberation and collaborative problem solving, a small percentage of citizens involved in public deliberation will be inspired and empowered to add new activities to their agenda (I estimate 5–10 percent, although I would like to research this at some point).

Now, even a handful of citizens who are newly activated in this sense can become a significant force for change on the level of their immediate community or as new players in larger networks. This in itself is a significant impact of public deliberation work. But most participants in public deliberation processes do not become community activists. Instead, they become more aware and confident citizens who have made some degree of progress toward public judgment on a particular issue. As such they are better able to inform and support relevant public policies. And, I suspect, they make many microadjustments in their attitudes and activities that contribute, slowly and surely, to important community impacts over time.

Civil society or other nongovernmental organizations involved in public deliberation efforts are in a parallel situation. That is, few are likely to take on entirely new initiatives as a result of their involvement (which certainly happens on occasion, but not typically). But many will adjust their ongoing activities in important ways as a result of what they learn or connections they make through deliberative political processes. They may decide, for instance, that some old, withering partnership can be revitalized by aligning it with an emerging community purpose and a sense of common ground.[10]

While the analysis of impact and power in this section applies to national politics as much as to local, the fact is that deliberative politics, especially in the United States, has had the greatest play and the greatest influence at the local level. Just so, the applied chapters in this book, as well as the larger literature, show the kinds of impacts discussed in this section primarily at the local level of politics and community life. Making this work meaningful at the national level is clearly a taller order. The remainder of this chapter explores this challenge, first as a general matter and then in light of the fresh possibilities stemming from the Obama presidency.

Exploring National Possibilities for Deliberative Politics

The problem that the size of the polity has posed for deliberative democracy has been recognized for virtually as long as the existence of political science, beginning with Aristotle's advice that polities function best when they are small enough that people can know one another and meet together. America's founders, of course, recognized the importance of deliberation to a successful democracy but concentrated the practice among the people's representatives, especially in the senate, rather than the general populace.[11]

Indeed, the notion of "mass deliberative politics" has the faint ring of an oxymoron, whereas other forms of politics, such as electoral, interest group, and movement politics, make more intuitive sense on a large scale. Citizens mobilize on a mass scale everyday in service to these kinds of political activities through mass media, the Internet, and various forms of organizing. But this kind of *mobilization* is quite different from a politics in which citizens, individually and collectively, contribute to public life by encountering issues and ideas in ways that help them work toward public judgment and various sorts of public action.

Such deliberative politics requires the creation of conditions and opportunities for citizen engagement, a kind of "democratic TLC" that differentiates it from other forms of politics more easily adapted to large-scale activity. And this is why deliberative public engagement is more easily accomplished within communities and on the level of local, "human-scale" politics than on the national level. But recognizing the challenge by no means implies that it is insurmountable.[12]

From Method to Strategy in Pursuit of a National Deliberative Politics

I suspect a major reason the deliberative democracy movement has struggled with the problem of scope is that our imaginations have been curtailed by the success we've had on the local level. We know how to create powerful deliberative forums within neighborhoods and communities. As a result, we naturally ask how we can "scale up" this activity and have a greater impact on national and international issues. I would suggest the very metaphor of "scaling up" is problematic, because it leads the field toward a kind of "super-size me" mentality that takes effective local methodologies and merely attempts to make them larger.

Such thinking could all too easily lead to projects that are prohibitively expensive (and all the more impractical in a time of economic distress) while also being prone to turning into another political spectacle—which, along with excessive polarization, appears to be the default setting of our national political culture. The unfortunate result could be the illusion of progress without substance. Worse yet, such grand deliberative ventures would be vulnerable to massive co-optation campaigns by well-funded special interests—witness the fate of the "town hall meetings" in our recent health care politics. However sincere the initial intent might be, such a fate could be exceedingly difficult to escape amid the hype and backroom power politics that could all too easily infect an extensive and expensive national forum exercise.

And even supposing that these dangers could be managed, it still strikes me that the notion of scaling up methods that have worked at the local level has short-circuited the field's ability to thinking broadly and *strategically*, rather than simply *methodologically*, about what a truly *national* deliberative politics might entail. Such a strategic approach, for instance, might look for ways to build on existing trends in a number of arenas in ways that would help make our society more deliberative in its very structures and culture. Three arenas that deserve special attention in this regard are the media, the worlds of school and work, and the manner in which deliberative work is done on the local level.

The Media's Role in a More Deliberative National Politics

As Habermas and many others have argued, the media play a critical role in the democratic process of any large polity. The current state of the media poses severe problems as a structural support for a more deliberative national polity, but it also offers significant opportunities that might be exploited.

Let's begin with an observation that Yankelovich makes in a number of places: while the news media tend to play a useful function during Stage 1 of the public judgment process (consciousness raising), they typically fall short during Stage 2 (working through and choice work).[13] This happens for a number of reasons: they're on to the next story; they provide more technical information than people can absorb; they polarize and sensationalize issues or become obsessed with "horse-race" reporting in ways that hinder working through rather than enhance it.

The "public journalism" movement tried to rectify this weakness by working for a press that was as responsive to the public's concerns as to the official policy agenda, and that attempted to play an active (but still non-partisan) role in supporting citizen understanding, dialogue, and problem solving.[14] To date, this movement has failed to gain much traction and has, if anything, lost ground (witness the demise of the Pew Center for Civic Journalism). In large part, it was beaten back by prominent traditionalists within the field, as in this example:

> For many of the country's leading journalists, the idea of public journalism rings false. Rosen quotes Leonard Downie, executive editor of *The Washington Post*, who has argued that public journalism oversteps the bounds of good reporting "by forcing candidates to participate in dialogues with voters, by staging campaign events, by deciding what good citizenship is and force-feeding it to citizens and voters, by pressuring citizens to register and vote when, as I say, nonvoting can also be viewed as an honorable and honest way to participate in the democratic process." Influential journalists from *The New York Times* have been more scathing. In a signed "Editorial Notebook" article, Howell Raines, *The Times*'s editorial page editor, said James Fallows's much-discussed 1996 book, "Breaking the News," posed an "insidious danger, and that is that reporters and editors become public policy missionaries with a puritanical contempt for horse-race politics."[15]

Another likely factor in civic journalism's lost momentum, and certainly another contributor to the news media's inability to support public judgment in our era even if its practitioners wanted to, is the stark fact that traditional news media are weakening, if not heading for outright extinction. Most notably, this can be seen in the death of newspapers around the country. In their place is the rise of niche outlets, including much of the ideologically extreme persuasion found on talk radio and cable news. While these media do encourage a sort of citizen engagement, they clearly work against national dialogue and deliberation by reinforcing people's preexisting views and hardening them against giving others a fair hearing.[16]

The last point notwithstanding, web-based "new media" remain a wild card in the possibility for a healthier public sphere more conducive to citizen judgment on pressing public problems. The Internet has certainly become key to any effort at mass politics, deliberative or otherwise. It has democratized access to information, and if information alone were a means to public judgment, a national, deliberative political culture might already have taken root. Indeed, the fact that such a culture hasn't emerged reinforces Yankelovich's point that information is overrated as a key to a more deliberative polity—that it is, essentially, a necessary but insufficient factor.

In addition to disseminating information, the Internet has proven itself to be a powerful platform for enabling social networks. But like cable news and talk radio, the Internet appears, so far at least, to be a powerful means to link people with similar perspectives. It less often brings together people of different perspectives and persuasions in dialogic and learning processes. Whether (or more hopefully, how) it can become a platform to help diverse citizens consider diverse ideas and develop a sense of public judgment remains to be seen.

Still, given the weakening of the traditional media gatekeepers who effectively short-circuited the public journalism movement, and given the rapid spread and evolution of highly flexible web-based platforms, it is certainly possible that new web-based media could evolve that could have a huge impact on our society's ability to support public judgment and citizen engagement. Strategically, it certainly makes sense for deliberative democracy researchers and practitioners to pay a great deal of critical attention to how web-based media can play a growing role in citizen engagement and public judgment, and many are doing exactly that. [17]

The Institutions That Touch Us All:
The Worlds of School and Work

Deliberative new-media experiments will only morph and expand into a media environment conducive to a deliberative style of politics if there is a demand for it that would make business models workable or public investments defendable. How will such demand come into being?

Sometimes, new products and platforms create their own markets as they burst onto the scene and spread in mysterious, viral ways. It is conceivable that some new deliberative democratic web-based application will awaken citizens to the need for a media more conducive to and supportive of public judgment. But there's no good reason to tether all our hopes for a ramped-up demand for a more deliberative democratic politics to such unpredictable phenomena. If we are convinced that this is the direction our society and politics need to go, then we should also look to the places in our society that help shape our political character. And within those places, we should look for trends we can build on to nurture a more deliberative sensibility and set of capacities among our citizens.

The skills and "habits of the heart" that citizens must develop in order to engage public issues effectively can be developed in many settings, not exclusively community forums or new online communities and processes. Schools that engage students in democratic decision making are one example. Another is the workplace, which can offer an important training ground for deliberative democratic skill building. And since these are the institutions that touch virtually all of us, they should be an important focus for any strategy devoted to bringing a more deliberative national politics into being.

In the educational arena, important current efforts include the work of CIRCLE (Center for Information and Research on Civic Learning and Engagement), the National Conference on Citizenship, and the Service Learning movement. Each reflects the Jeffersonian vision of an informed, educated, and participatory citizenry as the bulwark against government abuse of power and the source of renewal within our communities and nation. Expanding and strengthening these sorts of efforts—and especially ensuring that they pay attention to nurturing a capacity for civic dialogue and deliberation of the sort that builds public judgment—will be one important path to a new national politics.

There are other trends within education to build on, perhaps even more powerful ones. In particular, there is a strong argument within the worlds of education and workforce development that the curriculum and teaching methodologies that worked well for the twentieth-century industrial economy are poorly suited to preparing students for success in twenty-first-century jobs and the knowledge economy. This is reflected in an increasing emphasis on STEM (science, technology, engineering, and math) education and, especially, the related notion of twenty-first-century job skills like critical thinking and teamwork. These sorts of cognitive and social skills of analysis, problem solving, and collaboration are directly related to, and often identical with, the skills of a deliberative citizenry. Thus, the *economic* imperatives that are slowly changing what and how schools teach and students learn are also driving American education toward nurturing the skill set of deliberative democratic citizenship. This is therefore a trend to be doubly supported.

Related to this trend, and much less frequently discussed as a potential source of democratic renewal, is another institution that touches just about everyone: work. This is where people spend most of their time (Americans more than most!), and it seems likely that the ways in which workplace decisions are made, how employees are viewed and treated, and the nature of people's day-to-day activities all play a role in reinforcing attitudes and sharpening skills that are relevant to one kind of politics or another.

More specifically, it is likely that workplaces with relatively democratic cultures and practices help workers develop attitudes and skills that support deliberative politics. I found evidence of this in research I conducted a number of years ago with employees at an electric power plant that had established a very robust culture of teamwork and employee engagement. [18] My objective was to explore the possibility that *employee* engagement might nurture attitudes and skills that could be applied to *community* engagement and deliberative problem solving. The research, while limited in scope, strongly suggested that this can indeed be the case.

Consider these interview quotes from plant workers about how the skills of teamwork and problem solving within the plant were having an impact on their community lives:

> I've been able to use some of the skills I've learned [in the plant] in church and different things I'm involved with. Especially helping people get organized, and facilitating things. . . . People have a tendency to jump right into the nuts and bolts of things. We have been taught [at work] to take a step back and decide what the purpose is of what we are doing here.

> Everybody works together now, and it's helped me communicate better with everybody and be more outspoken than I used to be, including in the community.

Commenting on a specific initiative in which the plant partnered with local schools to improve science and math educational opportunities, plant workers said this:

> Both sides have to be willing to listen and give up some of their thinking that they're right and their egos.

> In the end you come up with something that everybody has worked on together. . . . We all sat there and experienced the pain of hammering this out together and came away with something that we all agreed on.

More research is needed on this topic, but this project suggested to me that workplaces emphasizing employee engagement, empowerment, and teamwork are important not only because they create highly productive commercial enterprises and enhanced worker satisfaction, but also because they promote democratic skills and a sense of "deliberative efficacy."

Local Capacity as a Stepping-Stone to National Deliberative Politics

High-quality, local public engagement is a critical step toward mass deliberative politics. This is the case, first, because it gives citizens a taste for a new kind of politics more satisfying than political business as usual, thus reinforcing the demand and citizen-capacity factor discussed in the last section.[19]

Moreover, as argued earlier, deliberative public engagement should generally (though not necessarily always) aim for two main goals. The first is achieving progress on concrete issues that affect people's well-being; and embedding capacity for future deliberative problem solving in governmental institutions, nongovernmental organizations, and grassroots groups. The second goal is important not only to the development of local communities, but also as a means to build a foundation for a national deliberative politics by establishing more capacity for citizen engagement in more places.

As public officials, civil society organizations, and grassroots leaders in communities across the nation learn to apply the principles and strategies that bring citizens and leaders together to solve local problems, and as more citizens participate, the practices of deliberative democracy will become more embedded in local political cultures. As a result, more communities, organizations, and associations will be enabled to become potential nodes or hubs within a national network, which over time can become the infrastructure for a truly national deliberative politics.

This need not mean that these hubs will join in a centrally organized national deliberation on a specific issue. That could certainly occur, but it would also be a good step if there were simply many more deliberative public conversations on a variety of important issues taking place across the nation, accruing toward more public judgment and a more generally deliberatively engaged citizenry. And if such local hubs became experienced and "tough" enough to resist co-optation and other forms of corruption or undermining on the local level, the goal of truly national and relatively synchronous citizen engagement on specific critical national issues becomes more likely to reach.

One promising trend in this regard is that national networks of civil society organizations, such as the League of Women Voters, the United Way, the National League of Cities, and many others, are increasingly embracing deliberative politics as part of their work. As a result they are supporting their local chapters or members to act as nonpartisan conveners for citizen engagement and helping them create capacity for this role, raising the prospect for a truly national infrastructure of know-how and venues. This is also occurring among informal national networks, such as libraries (some of which belong to the National Issues Forums network) and institutions of higher education.[20] Add to this the fact that we're in the early stages of national network creation by various public engagement organizations.[21] These phenomena, taken as a whole, make truly national efforts to deliberatively engage citizens around tough issues increasingly possible to imagine.

All these trends offer strategic possibilities for transforming the current dissatisfaction with take-no-prisoners partisanship into a demand for something more inclusive and constructive, which is, in part, the current that bore Barack Obama to office. As a prelude to considering the significance of the Obama moment for a more deliberative national politics, I'll discuss the challenges that deliberative democratic leadership poses for *any* public official and the resistances and ambivalences such leaders must contend with.

Paradoxes of Deliberative Democratic Leadership

For Yankelovich, perhaps *the* key to facilitating public judgment on any level of politics and public life is to encourage and educate leaders to do more things that accelerate the public's learning curve and fewer things that obstruct it. Indeed, Yankelovich in *Coming to Public Judgment* frames his entire project as one of establishing the right relationship between leaders and the public: "When the proper balance exists between the public and the nation's elites, our democracy works beautifully. When that balance is badly skewed, as in the present era, the system malfunctions. The chief symptom is the nation's inability to arrive at consensus on how to cope with its . . . most urgent problems."[22] Simply put, leaders are crucial to bringing about public judgment because they are in the best position to communicate with citizens in ways that support it. Thus: "In a democracy, the function of leadership is to alert the public to the existence of any serious threat, define it, develop strategy (or alternative strategies) for dealing with it, and seek to mobilize and focus the energies of the people to meet it."[23]

By this account, not only are leaders well positioned to promote public judgment, but it is in their interest as decision makers to do so. When the public is more deliberative and has come to terms with an issue, leaders are less subject to the chaotic gusts of public opinion and more able to navigate the steady currents of judgment. How exactly the nation gets to where it is going, the steps it must take along the way, and the unexpected turbulences it must negotiate can be left in the experienced hands of experts. But the general direction of where we're going, based on the values we care about as a people and the trade-offs we are willing to accept, can be stably set only by an engaged, responsible public.

Yankelovich acknowledges, however, that leaders do in fact often work against, rather than for, public judgment. He notes, for instance, that "the immense effort required to develop public judgment discourages most policy makers, who would rather deal with their fellow elites than with the public."[24] To remedy this problem, he recommends that we rethink the notion of leadership and how to nurture it to include what might be called "deliberative democratic leadership" alongside other types, styles, and functions:

> Literature on leadership is vast but seldom does it focus on the leader as a person who helps to shape public judgment. . . . It should be clear that the two alternatives of slavishly following the opinion polls or standing on one's own convictions irrespective of public opinion are false choices for a democracy. In a democracy, one of the major qualifications of leaders is that they develop the skill to move the public toward consensus by playing a constructive role at every stage of the public judgment process—consciousness raising, working through, and resolution. For this to happen, the culture has to broaden its definition of leadership to incorporate this ability.[25]

All of this makes perfect sense as far as it goes. But it also skips over a great deal of important messiness that must be sorted through if political leaders in particular are to serve such a constructive function vis-à-vis the public's process of coming to judgment. Before we can hope to see leaders play the vital role assigned them by Yankelovich, we need to understand the cross-cutting and sometimes perverse incentives officials face with respect to actively supporting public judgment and the ambivalence, if not outright resistance, this can create in them. Only when we understand *why* deliberative democratic leadership is so tricky will we be in a better position to motivate, support, and strengthen it, and also to compensate for its inevitable lapses.

Controlling Public Opinion versus Supporting Public Judgment: A Fundamental Tension

In general, the competitive, partisan, special interest–saturated environment in which public officials operate is more likely to drive them to try to dominate the public debate than to nurture public judgment. The latter requires a letting go of control that can be quite uncomfortable and unnatural for political elites. It is, after all, rarely what brought them to power, and it can be hard to explain to one's political backers, whose support was typically won by a commitment to a particular policy agenda rather than to an open political process. Exacerbating the problem is how little most political leaders know about deliberative democracy and how many lousy memories they have of painful and unproductive public hearings.

Yet, as Yankelovich explains, from the perspective of public judgment, opening up the public debate and letting go of a measure of control is exactly what needs to happen: "At a certain point, leaders must let go. For democracy to work the leader's arguments and persuasion and arm twisting must come to an end and the work of the citizens must begin. That work consists of weighing the leaders' recommendations against alternative choices. One of the critical stages in democracy comes when the 'choice work' is transferred from leaders to the public."[26]

Ideally this is so, but as political communications scholar Robert Entman notes, "Elites who want to succeed politically cannot afford to debate complicated truths in a marketplace of ideas."[27] Most typically, they (or their political operatives) view themselves as managers of public opinion and not as nonpartisan civic educators. They seek to make their version of events matter most in the mind of citizens by controlling the way media and citizens frame it. They seek, in other words, to dominate the debate rather than to stimulate it; to persuade and, in a sense, to end thought, not to engage and provoke it. And the higher up in political power one goes, the more this seems to be true. Thus, in the formulation of one student of the presidency, that office holder seeks to be—and often is—the "interpreter-in-chief."[28]

A Growing Appreciation by Public Officials

To recognize that public officials are often ambivalent about authentic public deliberation does not mean they are inevitably opposed to it or unable to help lead it. Certainly, on the level of local politics there is mounting evidence of a growing number of public officials who have decided that engaging citizens about solutions is a critical dimension of effective and legitimate governance.

At Public Agenda, we've seen this occur in the course of our long history of work on education reform, as recounted in Chapter 4. This was just one example of a wider phenomenon that is well documented by Matt Leighninger in his *The Next Form of Democracy*, among others.[29] The growing list of public officials, on the local level especially, who are involved with innovative and inclusive forms of citizen engagement is a hopeful sign that our democratic norms and practices are evolving.

On the national level, there has also been some significant commitment to public participation in public policy development in several federal agencies—often in spite of, rather than because of, federal guidelines requiring some type of formal public input.[30] And there have even been times when presidents have decided to stimulate public deliberation rather than control public opinion. The Clinton administration's call in 1998 for a national dialogue on Social Security was an example:

> So the question is what is the fairest way to change [Social Security]? What's best for people who are on Social Security now? What's best for the baby boomers? What's best for young people in their 20s and 30s just starting to pay into the system? What's best for the kids that are in high school now who haven't even started?
>
> We're going to spend a year having forums all across the country, completely non-partisan, trying to bring people in and debate it. And then about a year from now, I'm going to convene the leaders of Congress and we're going to try to craft historic bipartisan legislation to reform Social Security, to save it for the 21st century, to make sure it's there not just for the baby boomers, but for everybody in this audience and all your children, too, so we'll have a system that works, so that people who work hard and do their part will know they'll have elemental retirement security and that we can do it without bankrupting the country. I think we can do it. I know we can do it. But it's going to take your good-faith involvement—people of all ages.[31]

A major national effort took place at the time to engage citizens across the county in deliberation on Social Security, funded by the Pew Charitable Trust and carried out by the nonpartisan citizen engagement organization America Speaks. While this initiative did not result in policy reform, it did engage about fifty thousand Americans in considering an important public problem, and it exposed many executive branch and congressional officials to what public deliberation looks like and to the considered views of a large cross section of the citizenry.[32]

The specific impacts of this initiative aside, this instance illustrates the broader point that there are political moments when it can make sense to even national politicians to open up and support—rather than control—a robust, citizen-centered, nonpartisan, public policy dialogue.[33] Clearly, something interesting and complex is brewing on this front with the Obama administration.

Obama and the Possibilities
for a More Deliberative National Politics

Among the reasons Obama came to power was his team's ability to actively engage and empower large numbers of citizen volunteers, and to inspire many more with the possibility of a more inclusive and pragmatic political process. Once in power, the new administration has made some important moves toward greater transparency and openness, and Obama has exhibited a rhetorical and leadership style that bodes well for those who seek a politics more rooted in public judgment.

However, these acts and impulses have been complicated by ambivalences, confusions, and crosscurrents of the very sort that I discussed in the previous section. Thus, while there is much that is fresh, hopeful, and worthy of support in the president's approach, we should not be naive and starry-eyed about being on the brink of a post-partisan age of citizen-centered national politics. Rather, there are two questions that confront us: What significant advances can we reasonably strive to make at this important juncture, and what dangers must we avoid as we endeavor to do so?

Some Hopeful Signs

It was encouraging that even before the inauguration, the president-elect and his team were not only calling on citizens to weigh in on national issues and to volunteer and organize to address local concerns, but also providing practical tools to help Americans get organized, including web-based platforms to enable them to provide policy input or organize meetings with their neighbors, and guides that people could use at gatherings to help promote open, productive conversation about significant public issues.[34]

Another noteworthy early development was the memorandum signed by President Obama on his second day in office directing the heads of executive departments and agencies to better inform and engage the public. Not only did the memo call for more transparency, it also directed officials to make government more "participatory," arguing that "public engagement enhances the Government's effectiveness and improves the quality of its decisions." Moreover—and here we see a glimmer of something genuinely innovative—it calls on executive departments and agencies to "solicit public input on how we can increase and improve opportunities for public participation."[35] This suggested not only a seriousness of purpose but a refreshing openness to the kind of democratic innovation needed to contribute to the solutions that we must, collectively, bring into being.

There have also been a number of online platforms to solicit ideas from citizens and groups on a number of questions, including how to improve the administration's ability to engage the citizenry on public policy or governmental practice questions. And possibly one of Obama's strongest contributions to date toward a more deliberative public discourse is his pragmatic and inclusive rhetorical style, which was on clear display in his September 9, 2009, health care speech before Congress, after a summer of sharply ideological political warfare.

> There are those on the left who believe that the only way to fix the system is through a single-payer system like Canada's where we would severely restrict the private insurance market and have the government provide coverage for everybody. On the right, there are those who argue that we should end employer-based systems and leave individuals to buy health insurance on their own.
>
> I've said—I have to say that there are arguments to be made for both these approaches. But either one would represent a radical shift that would disrupt the health care most people currently have. Since health care represents one-sixth of our economy, I believe it makes more sense to build on what works and fix what doesn't, rather than try to build an entirely new system from scratch. (Applause.) And that is precisely what those of you in Congress have tried to do over the past several months.
>
> During that time, we've seen Washington at its best and at its worst.
>
> We've seen many in this chamber work tirelessly for the better part of this year to offer thoughtful ideas about how to achieve reform. Of the five committees asked to develop bills, four have completed their work, and the Senate Finance Committee announced today that it will move forward next week. That has never happened before. Our overall efforts have been supported by an unprecedented coalition of doctors and nurses; hospitals, seniors' groups, and even drug companies—many of whom opposed reform in the past. And there is agreement in this chamber on about 80 percent of what needs to be done, putting us closer to the goal of reform than we have ever been.
>
> But what we've also seen in these last months is the same partisan spectacle that only hardens the disdain many Americans have towards their own government. Instead of honest debate, we've seen scare tactics. Some have dug into unyielding ideological camps that offer no hope of compromise. Too many have used this as an opportunity to score short-term political points, even if it robs the country of our opportunity to solve a long-term challenge. And out of this blizzard of charges and counter-charges, confusion has reigned.
>
> Well, the time for bickering is over. The time for games has passed.

Now is the season for action. Now is when we must bring the best ideas of both parties together, and show the American people that we can still do what we were sent here to do.[36]

All these elements of the Obama presidency (transparency, online platforms, a pragmatic, problem-solving rhetorical style) provide deliberative democrats with grounds for hope and with opportunities—but the picture is by no means a simple one.

Complications of a Deliberative Presidency

Alongside such attempts to establish a national politics that is open to broad-based public judgment and citizen input has been a more traditional politics of mobilization that seeks to rally citizens around a specific legislative agenda. To be as clear as I can be, and as I hope my earlier discussion of public officials and public engagement showed, I do not consider this to be wrong but rather an inevitable and tricky dynamic of deliberative leadership by public officials.

An important instance of how the impulse toward advocacy and mobilization complicates and sometimes supersedes the possibilities for broad-based public deliberation was the transformation of the Obama campaign's grassroots network into the Organizing for America entity, which was then placed under the aegis of the Democratic National Committee (DNC). Now, it's true that the administration had to remove this citizen engagement and mobilization vehicle from the White House, because the e-mail list at its heart was compiled for campaign purposes and using it as a White House governance tool would violate the rules. But a less partisan and narrowly political setting than the DNC would have been more promising from the standpoint of a more deliberative democracy that supports broad-based public judgment.

Again, such developments should not surprise or even disappoint us. The president, after all, came to power on a party platform in a partisan election. The powerful pull of policy and political exigencies was bound to bend the president's more inclusive, deliberative, and citizen-centered impulses toward frank partisan politics, at least to a degree. To the extent that Obama was elected to enact *both* a better political process *and* a particular agenda meant there were bound to be tensions between these two poles of his presidency.

Further complicating the picture are efforts to engage citizens that seem to have had perfectly good intentions but fell short because of weaknesses in design and technique. Some of the online input efforts can be put in this category. A number of these efforts have generated some ideas and decent discussion but, unfortunately, far too much off-topic advocacy for things like marijuana legalization (not the topic at hand) or ranting about supposed mysteries surrounding Obama's birth certificate (ditto). These are the perfect example of what happens when leaders open up channels of citizen input without creating conditions for citizen judgment.

The "town hall" meetings on health care also deserve prominent mention here. These were particularly frustrating to those of us who have been working on the challenges of deliberative forum design for many years. The health care town halls of the summer of 2009 were, in the end, weak attempts to provide minimally deliberative opportunities for citizens to learn more about health care and to engage their leaders on the subject. There was at least a degree of authenticity to them in that participants were not pre-screened and the proceedings were not overly controlled. But they were so poorly designed that their very openness allowed them to be hijacked by the loudest and angriest voices. [37]

Toward Greater Clarity

The situation is also tricky for deliberative democracy advocates, who must support the new administration's more democratic impulses without being partisan about them (any knee-jerk partisanship defeats our purpose) and without being naively shocked when the president eschews nonpartisan leadership in order to actively push his policy agenda. There's much to sort out here, but it's a rather new and refreshing challenge to face, and one that we should welcome.

One thing we can ask of the administration, it seems to me, is that when the president does act in a partisan mode, he avoid the temptations of partisanship for its own sake and the destructive rhetoric that makes inclusive and pragmatic problem solving so difficult to achieve. Fortunately, President Obama has shown an unusual ability to disagree without being disagreeable and to argue for his own agenda while respecting others' points of view—as in the health care speech quoted earlier. In doing so, he is modeling a style of engagement and argument that our political culture sorely needs.

The other important danger we must watch carefully is that of the administration blurring the line (whether intentionally or simply out of confusion) between nonpartisan public engagement and partisan mobilization, which could end up compromising both. In addition to Organizing for America discussed earlier, another case in point is the rechristening of the presidential office of public liaison (which manages interest group and constituency relations) as the office of public engagement. So far, this development appears to reflect a rhetorical shift more than an actual change in the office's purpose and function. On the other hand, the fact that officials from this office have spent significant time exposing themselves to deliberative democratic thinkers and practitioners is encouraging and suggests at least the possibility that the office might broaden its democratic function over time.

The bottom line here is that if the administration is comfortable engaging citizens across the political spectrum on a particular issue and encouraging pragmatic rather than ideological solutions, that should be considered a real and refreshing plus. And if the administration is dealing with an issue on which it decides it must take a partisan stand, that is also fine. The problem comes for those of us concerned about bringing into being a more deliberative democratic process when partisan work is dressed up in nonpartisan clothing, because this eats away at the credibility and effectiveness of the work.

While part of the answer here is to support the administration when it is in inclusive public deliberation mode and to promote real clarity when it is not, another part is to balance official leadership for public judgment with nonofficial leadership.

Why Nongovernmental Leadership for Public Judgment Will Always Be Needed

That a growing number of public officials, certainly on the local level and to some extent nationally as well, support a more engaged and deliberative public is certainly a positive sign. In this, public officials are on their own "learning curve," discovering that the public is a resource and potential partner and not just a problem to be managed, and that there are more constructive ways of engaging the citizenry than they have previously experienced through traditional interest group politics or painful and futile public hearing processes.

But public officials should not be the only ones who support and facilitate public engagement and judgment. Nongovernmental leadership will always be needed as well, for a number of reasons. This leadership can come from quasi-official neighborhood and school councils, or from nonofficial entities such as schools and colleges, the League of Women Voters, the United Way, book clubs, news outlets, church groups, online communities, and nonpartisan civic engagement organizations (such as those featured in this volume and many others).

Nongovernmental leadership for public deliberation is critical, first, because public resources for this work will be limited for the foreseeable future and because we can't reach the critical mass of citizens and communities required for a national deliberative politics unless many actors from many sectors support it. But that's not the only reason. It is essential as well in order to enable the public to address important issues that public officials are unwilling to open up to public dialogue and engagement.

Even if a public official has come to understand the advantages of engaging the citizenry and supporting public judgment, and even if that official begins to develop the knowledge and capacity to do so productively, there will be issues that he or she will resist "letting go" of in the sense that Yankelovich says must occur so that the public can do its work. For instance, a politician who has always fought against school vouchers and has succeeded electorally because of this position is unlikely to lead an open public conversation on whether or not vouchers are a good idea. He or she might be a perfectly fine *participant* in an engagement process on the topic, but other actors will typically have to lead that conversation if it is to have real democratic credibility and impact.

Moreover, some issues are simply outside the mainstream political agenda, and thus unlikely to be supported by public officials as appropriate topics for public conversation, but they are still vitally important. Until recently, for instance, it would have been hard to imagine more than a few public officials at any level willing to help lead a public engagement process on the topic of gay marriage. But that doesn't mean it should not have happened. It's been a simmering social issue, fighting its way onto the public agenda and erupting in movement politics and legal skirmishes, but the public has not had nearly the opportunity it needs to really think it through by looking at it from different perspectives and talking to people with different experiences and points of view. As a result, gay marriage has become a wedge issue in electoral battles rather than being regarded as an important public question requiring careful consideration from many viewpoints and meriting a serious attempt at problem solving.

Finally, the skepticism with which the American people tend to look at government means that individuals other than public officials will need to be players in public deliberation processes in order for citizens to trust them sufficiently that they can be meaningful and legitimate forces in public life. This skepticism has worsened in recent generations, and some measure of public trust can surely be recovered. But a degree of healthy wariness toward the abuse of power has been part of the nation's political culture from the beginning, as in Madison's timeless argument in number 51 of the *Federalist Papers:*

> If men were angels, no government would be necessary. If angels were to govern men, neither external nor internal controls on government would be necessary. In framing a government which is to be administered by men over men, the great difficulty lies in this: you must first enable the government to control the governed; and in the next place oblige it to control itself. A dependence on the people is, no doubt, the primary control on the government; but experience has taught mankind the necessity of auxiliary precautions.

I doubt this skeptical edge in America's political sensibility will ever die away completely, and I doubt as well that it ever should. Given this reality, civil society will always be an important source for deliberative leadership and democratic renewal.

Looking closely at the public judgment framework and what we have learned about its practical application over the years brings us to questions on the cutting edge of deliberative democracy—questions about power and impact, scope and political culture, leadership and citizenship. These are the issues that the larger field must wrestle with if it is to continue to progress from a constructive but limited phenomenon on the periphery of American public life to become a central and powerful force for a more inclusive, pragmatic, just, and meaningful democratic process.

Notes

Foreword

1. John Diaz, *San Francisco Chronicle*, October 18, 2009.
2. Alexis de Tocqueville, *Democracy in America*, trans. Harvey C. Mansfield and Delba Winthrop (Chicago: University of Chicago Press, 2000), 499.

Introduction

1. Daniel Yankelovich, *Coming to Public Judgment: Making Democracy Work in a Complex World* (Syracuse, NY: Syracuse University Press, 1991).
2. The terms "coming to public judgment" and "the public's learning curve" are used more or less interchangeably throughout the book. The "learning curve" language is Yankelovich's preferred metaphor in recent years for the processes he first articulated in published form in *Coming to Public Judgment*. When authors of other chapters employ the language of public judgment, they are essentially covering the same ground.
3. While it's been almost twenty years since *Coming to Public Judgment* was published, two organizations represented in this book (Public Agenda and the Kettering Foundation, initiator of the National Issues Forums) were working with Yankelovich and the ideas about the public for many years prior to 1991.
4. In this they are working in the same general realm as Jim Fishkin (see, e.g., *The Voice of the People: Public Opinion and Democracy* [New Haven, CT: Yale University Press, 1995]), whose "deliberative polls" do related work. It is critical to the field that there be numerous experiments of this kind to drive theoretical and applied knowledge.

Chapter 1

1. John C. Bogle, "Stewardship vs. Salesmanship: Bond Mutual Funds Gone Awry" (address to Fixed Income Analysts Society, New York, April 17, 2007), at *johncbogle.com*.

2. See Martha C. Nussbaum, *Upheavals of Thought* (New York: Cambridge University Press, 2001).

3. Hilary Putnam, *The Collapse of the Fact/Value Dichotomy* (Cambridge, MA: Harvard University Press, 2002).

4. Daniel Goleman, *Emotional Intelligence* (New York: Bantam Books, 1997).

5. See especially Antonio Damasio, *Descartes' Error* (New York: Penguin Books, 1994).

Chapter 2

1. At some point in the 1990s, Public Agenda leadership dropped the use of "Foundation."

2. See Chapter 4 of this volume.

3. The Deliberative Democracy Consortium, the National Coalition for Dialogue and Deliberation, and Public Agenda's Center for Advances in Public Engagement are among the organizations making efforts to bridge academic researchers and practitioners in the larger deliberative democracy/public engagement movement.

4. Daniel Yankelovich, *The Magic of Dialogue: Transforming Conflict into Cooperation* (New York: Simon and Schuster, 1999).

Chapter 3

1. For background information on the National Issues Forums network and access to the many issue books that have been produced over the years, visit *www.nifi.org*.

2. Carmen Sirianni and Lewis Friedland, *Civic Innovation in America* (Berkeley: University of California Press, 2001), 1.

3. Benjamin Barber, "Neither Consent nor Dissent," *The American Prospect*, November 4, 2002.

4. Benjamin Barber, *Strong Democracy: Participatory Politics for a New Age* (Berkeley: University of California Press, 1985), 320.

5. Philip E. Converse, "The Nature of Belief Systems in Mass Publics," in *Ideology and Discontent*, ed. David E. Apter (New York: Free Press, 1964).

6. Bryan Caplan, *The Myth of the Rational Voter: Why Democracies Choose Bad Policies* (Princeton, NJ: Princeton University Press, 2007).

7. Yankelovich, *Coming to Public Judgment*, 239.

8. Sirianni and Friedland, "The Civic Renewal Movement," in *Civic Innovation in America*, 260.

Chapter 4

1. Phone interview of Deborah Wadsworth by Alison Kadlec, August 20, 2008.
2. In *Coming to Public Judgment*, Yankelovich compares the role of information in public opinion formation to the role that memory plays for a great pianist. While memory is certainly indispensable for the pianist, it is obviously not sufficient. He goes on to say, "I am not denigrating information anymore than I would be denigrating memory by pointing to the qualities of creativity, technique, and feeling that make for greatness in a pianist" (Yankelovich, *Coming to Public Judgment*, 45). The point here is that the quality of information is vital to the public's ability to work through an issue and come to sound judgment, but it is neither sufficient nor necessarily the most important factor. To view information as the basis of knowledge makes sense for experts, but it is not the best way to understand how nonexperts think and generate knowledge. To expect the public to have expert-level knowledge in order to make thoughtful decisions is to find the public permanently deficient and to overlook the unique kinds of knowledge the public brings to the table in the form of values and experience.
3. This is not to say that nonpartisan intermediary organizations did not previously exist, for it is clear that outfits like the National Civic League and League of Women Voters are just such examples. Public Agenda incorporated, in a central way, both a research capacity and deliberative democracy theory and practice to inform the way such an organization could function.
4. See Chapter 3 of this volume.
5. See Yankelovich, *Coming to Public Judgment*, chapter 12.
6. See, e.g., Jean Johnson and John Immerwahr, *First Things First: What Americans Expect from the Public Schools* (Public Agenda, 1993), and Jean Johnson et al., *Assignment Incomplete: The Unfinished Business of Education Reform* (Public Agenda, 1995). An important work around this time that connected research findings such as ours to the notion of community engagement was David Mathews, *Is There a Public for Public Schools?* (Dayton: Kettering Foundation, 1996).
7. See, e.g., Matt Leighninger, *The Next Form of Democracy* (Nashville: Vanderbilt University Press, 2006), and John Gastil and Peter Levine, eds., *The Deliberative Democracy Handbook* (San Francisco: Jossey-Bass, 2005).
8. We argue this point in some depth in Alison Kadlec and Will Friedman, "Deliberative Democracy and the Problem of Power" (*Journal of Public Deliberation* 3, no. 1, 2007).
9. For examples of Public Agenda's Choicework Discussion Starters, go to *www .publicagenda.org/publicengagement/choicework-discussion-starters*. Yankelovich has been experimenting with this approach for many years, as have each of the organizations in the applied chapters of this volume; later in this chapter we

will discuss some formal research we've conducted on it. This does not mean we believe it is always the right approach to presenting issues to citizens—just that it's a very strong one with a lot of field experience behind it.

10. While some may associate the term "stakeholder" with a small, exclusive set of decision makers, we view the term more broadly and, perhaps, literally. For us, stakeholders are those who have a particular stake in an issue, and they include members of the general public.

11. There is a rather large issue for the deliberative democracy/public engagement field lurking behind our comments here, namely that of random sampling versus other strategies and frameworks for recruiting participants to deliberative processes. We have decided that the topic is too large and complex to address here and may turn to it in a future CAPE publication. For now, we'll say that our practice to date has been to use random sampling methodologies when we do formal research on public attitudes and thinking, and a stakeholder cross-section framework for our public engagement/ problem-solving work in communities. (Note that for us, stakeholders almost always include the general public and traditionally marginalized groups.) We believe that both random-sample and stakeholder perspectives are important to our overall mission of facilitating public judgment and bridging the gaps between citizens and leaders.

12. Some of the outcomes and actions flowing from Community Conversation work will be discussed in case examples later in this chapter. Others may be found in Will Friedman, *Changing the Conversation on Education in Connecticut* (Center for Advances in Public Engagement at Public Agenda, 2004), and Leighninger, *The Next Form of Democracy*.

13. This section draws heavily on Will Friedman, Alison Kadlec, and Lara Birnback, *Transforming Public Life: A Decade of Public Engagement in Bridgeport, CT* (Center for Advances in Public Engagement at Public Agenda, 2007). For another study of public engagement in Bridgeport, see Elena Fagotto and Archon Fung, *Embedded Deliberation: Entrepreneurs, Organizations, and Public Action: Final Report for the William and Flora Hewlett Foundation* (Taubman Center for State and Local Government, John F. Kennedy School of Government, Harvard University, 2006).

14. Friedman, *Changing the Conversation on Education in Connecticut.*

15. See Fagotto and Fung, *Embedded Deliberation.*

16. We encountered the same difficulties in our own research: many of those we spoke with talked about the regularity of Community Conversations and the different spin-offs from the original model, but no one seemed able to give a final accounting of the number of Conversations or the topics discussed. Quite possibly, the point at which community members cannot keep up with all the engagement activities taking place in their community should

be counted as a threshold indicator of "embeddedness." At this point the Community Conversation is no longer an unusual event; it has become part of the way things are done. Bridgeport's capacity for this work has developed to the point where a cadre of trained moderators and recorders are essentially on call.

17. Fagotto and Fung, *Embedded Deliberation*, 6.

18. Ibid., 20.

19. All quotes in this section are from Friedman, Kadlec, and Birnback, *Transforming Public Life*.

20. Fagotto and Fung, *Embedded Deliberation*, 27.

21. Ibid., 27.

22. Friedman, Kadlec, and Birnback, *Transforming Public Life*, 7.

23. Robert D. Putnam, "Community-Based Social Capital and Educational Performance," in *Making Good Citizens: Education and Civil Society*, ed. Diane Ravitch and Joseph P. Viteritti (New Haven, CT: Yale University Press, 2001), 69–72.

24. Alison Kadlec and Will Friedman, with Amber Ott, *Important, but Not for Me* (Public Agenda, 2007).

25. The memo is available from the authors by e-mailing them at *info@ publicagenda.org*.

26. Indeed, as it happened, Yankelovich took a direct hand in the research design, something he does only rarely at Public Agenda these days.

27. This book is itself a CAPE project. For more information, go to *www.publicagenda.org/cape*.

28. As Friedman explains, "framing to persuade" involves defining an issue to one's advantage in the hope of getting an audience to do what you want it to do. "Framing for deliberation," by contrast, involves clarifying the range of positions surrounding an issue so that citizens can better decide what they want to do. See Will Friedman, *Reframing Framing* (Center for Advances in Public Engagement at Public Agenda, 2007). For an overview of relevant literature, see S. D. Reese, O. H. Gandy Jr., and A. E. Grant, eds., *Framing Public Life: Perspectives on Media and Our Understanding of the Social World* (Philadelphia: Lawrence Erlbaum Associates, 2001). See also G. Lakoff, "Language and Woman's Place," in *Language in Society* (Cambridge: Cambridge University Press, 2008); G. Lakoff, *Moral Politics* (Chicago: University of Chicago Press, 2002); R. Entman, "Freezing Out the Public: Elite and Media Framing of the U.S. Anti-nuclear Movement," *Political Communication* 10, no. 2 (1993): 155–73; J. Druckman, "A Theory of Framing and Opinion Formation in Competitive Elite Environments," *Journal of Communication* 57, no. 1 (2007): 99–118; and J. Druckman, "Framing and Deliberation: How Citizens' Conversations Limit Elite Influence," *American Journal of Political Science* 47, no. 4 (2003): 729–45.

29. A full report on this research is forthcoming from CAPE. Here we discuss preliminary results.

Chapter 5

1. See, for example, Steven A. Rosell, *Renewing Governance: Governing by Learning in the Information Age* (New York: Oxford University Press, 1999).
2. This is described in detail in Yankelovich, *The Magic of Dialogue.* While this chapter summarizes work we have done in the public sphere, applying dialogue to advance the process of working through in order to develop more reliable opinion research and more effective governance, we have also applied our dialogue-based methods to the private sector. See, for example, Daniel Yankelovich and Steven Rosell, "Creating Strategic Dialogue," in *The Financial Times Handbook of Management*, 3rd ed. (Upper Saddle River, NJ: Prentice Hall, 2004), 851–55.
3. For a more detailed description of this project, see J. Maxwell, S. Rosell, and P. Forest, "Giving Citizens a Voice in Health Care Policy in Canada," *British Medical Journal* 326 (2003): 1031–33.
4. The report of the original project, *Listening to Californians: Bridging the Disconnect*, can be found at *www.ViewpointLearning.com*, along with reports on three follow-up projects: *Moving along the Learning Curve: Citizen Dialogues on K–12 Education; Health Coverage for All Californians: Catching Up with the Public*; and *Beyond Wishful Thinking: Californians Deliberate State Budget Reform*.
5. Additional information can be found on the project website, at *www.voicesforhealthcare.org*. Once this project is complete, a report will be available on the Viewpoint Learning website, at *www.ViewpointLearning.com*.
6. Interactive Briefings are designed not only to present findings but also to engage leaders in working through their implications and defining practical next steps.

Chapter 6

1. Yankelovich, *Coming to Public Judgment*, part 3.
2. Ibid., 116–17.
3. Ibid., 126–28.
4. Kadlec and Friedman, "Deliberative Democracy and the Problem of Power," 24. For related, excellent discussions, see Martin Carcasson, *Beginning with the End in Mind: A Call for Goal-Driven Deliberative Practice* (Center for Advances in Public Engagement at Public Agenda, 2009), and Xavier de Souza Briggs, *Democracy as Problem Solving* (Cambridge, MA: MIT Press, 2008).
5. Fagotto and Fung, *Embedded Deliberation.*

6. Deliberative capacity building on the local level is also important to the cause of an eventual national deliberative politics—more on this point later.

7. Public Agenda's case study of a decade of public deliberation in Bridgeport, Connecticut, illustrates impacts on concrete problems and community capacity building and on the roles played by civil society organizations (such as the Bridgeport Education Fund), public officials (such as the school superintendent), and individual citizens (including volunteers to work on community initiatives). See Friedman, Kadlec, and Birnback, *Transforming Public Life*.

8. For various examples of deliberative politics that are tied to concrete outcomes via the post-deliberation exercise of various forms of power, see Archon Fung, *Empowered Deliberation: Reinventing Urban Democracy* (Princeton, NJ: Princeton University Press, 2009).

9. Obama's speech on Guantanamo in spring 2009 is an interesting example, in which the president, noting that "there are no neat and easy answers here," talked through a series of tough decisions, some popular and some not, and the values conflicts inherent in them. See "Remarks by the President on National Security," National Archives, Washington, DC, May 21, 2009.

10. For an example, see Kadlec's and my discussion of Public Agenda's work in Kansas City in Chapter 4 of this volume.

11. Of the founders, Jefferson was one who imagined citizen deliberation and involvement in decision making, through a series of local assemblies or "ward meetings." See Jefferson's letter to John Adams of October 28, 1813, in Joyce Appleby and Terence Ball, eds., *Jefferson: Political Writings* (Cambridge: Cambridge University Press, 2003), 185–91.

12. Many strategies have been and are being attempted to "cope with scope" in deliberative politics, with varying degrees of success and lessons for future efforts, as I've discussed at some length in my essay "Deliberative Democracy and the Problem of Scope" (*Journal of Public Deliberation* 2, 2006).

13. "The media go for overkill in alerting the public to potential train wrecks, while offering very little help in averting them or preparing us to cope with them constructively" (Yankelovich, Chapter 1 of this volume).

14. See, e.g., Jay Rosen, *What Are Journalists For?* (New Haven, CT: Yale University Press, 1999).

15. Tom Goldstein, "Good Question" (review of Jay Rosen's *What Are Journalists For?, New York Times*, November 14, 1999).

16. For an experimental look at the kind of discussion of issues that is primed by cable-news type framing of issues versus the kind that emerges when issues are purposefully framed for deliberation, see Kadlec and Friedman, *Beyond Debate* (Center for Advances in Public Engagement at Public Agenda, 2009), as well as our summary of that research in Chapter 4 of this volume.

17. For a recent discussion of interesting efforts and experiments, see Scott Bittle, Chris Haller, and Alison Kadlec, *Promising Practices in Online Engagement* (Center for Advances in Public Engagement at Public Agenda, 2009). Various articles on the subject may also be found online in the *Journal of Public Deliberation* as well as at *www.virtualagora.org*. Finally, the Obama administration's efforts to engage citizens through the Internet are certainly promising and instructive; more on this later in the chapter.

18. For a fuller discussion, see Will Friedman, "From Employee Engagement to Civic Engagement: Exploring Connections between Workplace and Community Democracy" (*Kettering Review*, Kettering Foundation, Dayton, Ohio, 2009). The original research was conducted in 2002 and published through the now-defunct Work in America Institute.

19. I'm reminded of a Community Conversation that took place in the mid-1990s in the Crown Heights neighborhood of Brooklyn, New York, the site of a number of high-profile, tense episodes involving African American and Hasidic community members. This forum was organized around the issue of providing better educational opportunities to the neighborhood's children. The dialogue was exciting and deeply satisfying to the participants. One longtime resident commented as he walked out after lingering with the post-forum stragglers, "We should have done this twenty years ago."

20. On higher-education institutions, see Martin Carcasson (2009), *Democracy's Hubs: College and University Centers as Platforms for Deliberative Practice* (available from *mcarcas@colostate.edu*), as well as the higher-education initiative *The Democracy Imperative* (*www.unh.edu/democracy*).

21. Examples of forming public engagement networks include the National Coalition for Dialogue and Deliberation and the Deliberative Democracy Consortium, as well as the national networks of such organizations as America Speaks, Everyday Democracy, National Issues Forums, Public Agenda, and the Public Conversations Project.

22. Yankelovich, *Coming to Public Judgment*, 8.

23. Ibid., 101.

24. Ibid., 117.

25. Ibid., 243.

26. Ibid., 167.

27. Robert Entman, *Democracy without Citizens: Media and the Decay of American Politics* (New York: Oxford University Press, 1989). For an interesting older study that remains relevant here, see Benjamin Page, "The Theory of Political Ambiguity" (*American Political Science Review* 70, no. 3), 742–52.

28. M. Stuckey, *The President as Interpreter-in-Chief* (Chatham, NJ: Chatham House Publishers, 1991). On the distinction between framing for persuasion and framing for deliberation, see Friedman, "Reframing Framing."

29. Leighninger, *The Next Form of Democracy*. See also the National League of Cities' publication *Engaging Citizens in Public Works* (NLC, 2007); Sirianni and Friedland, *The Civic Renewal Movement*); de Souza Briggs, *Democracy as Problem Solving*; and many case studies by the Deliberative Democracy Consortium (at *www.deliberative-democracy.net*), the National Coalition for Dialogue and Deliberation (at *www.thataway.org*), and the International Association for Public Participation (at *www.iap2.Org/index.cfm*).

30. See, e.g., *Champions of Participation*, a 2009 report on a meeting of professionals from many federal agencies organized by America Speaks, Demos, Everyday Democracy, and the Ash Institute for Democratic Governance and Innovation (available at *www.americaspeaks.org*).

31. Bill Clinton, excerpts from president's speech in Champaign, Illinois, January 28, 1998 (Social Security Online: The Official Website of the U.S. Social Security Administration).

32. For more on the Americans Discuss Social Security initiative, go to *www.americaspeaks.org*.

33. Understanding the dynamics that lead national policy makers to decide it is particularly advantageous to open up public debate rather than try to control it could lead to a better reading of the opportunities for deliberative work.

34. Go to *www.mlkday.gov* for an example.

35. "Obama Memo on Transparency and Open Government" (Federal Register 74, no. 15, 2009), at *www.publicagenda.org/files/pdf/ObamaMemo OnTransparencyAndOpenGovernment.pdf*.

36. Office of the Press Secretary, "Remarks by the President to a Joint Session on Health Care," September 9, 2009, at *www.whitehouse.gov /the_press_office/Remarks-by-the-President-to-a-Joint-Session-of-Congress -on-Health-Care*.

37. It is instructive to compare the problems of "town hall meetings" during the George W. Bush years and the recent ones associated with Obama's health care reform efforts. The earlier events suffered from overcontrol, resulting in a canned, inauthentic display of public conversation that precluded the possibility of citizens learning about and working through the real trade-offs of different policy solutions. The recent town halls, meanwhile, suffered from the opposite malady of being underdesigned, making them vulnerable to all sorts of manipulative political theater as well as sincere but uncivil histrionics—with exactly the same sorry outcome for the public's ability to learn and develop judgment.

   To be clear, I am not in the least saying that those who oppose Obama's health care policies are manipulative or uncivil. I'm saying that the forums were so poorly designed, so lacking in basic deliberative democratic "best practices" that too much manipulation and incivility were able to find their way into the process and in the end, in many instances, dominate it. As a result, those who opposed the policies, those who supported them, and the many who were not sure about them had few opportunities to learn more, enter into deliberative give-and-take with leaders and fellow citizens, and otherwise consider the issue in ways that would further public judgment. For a discussion of the crucial role that good design plays in deliberative processes, see Kadlec and Friedman, "Deliberative Democracy and the Problem of Power."

Contributors

Will Friedman is president of Public Agenda. He joined the organization in 1994, became associate director of research in 1996, founded Public Agenda's public engagement department in 1997, and established the Center for Advances in Public Engagement in 2007. Previously, he was senior vice president for research and policy studies at the Work in America Institute. Among his many publications are "Deliberative Democracy and the Problem of Scope" and, with Alison Kadlec, "Deliberative Democracy and the Problem of Power." He holds a doctorate in political science and political psychology from the Graduate Center of the City University of New York.

Heidi Gantwerk is vice president of Viewpoint Learning, Inc., and specializes in civic engagement, public policy research, community relations, and media production. She has designed and directed civic and stakeholder engagement projects on a wide range of complex public and private sector issues, including health care reform, land use and housing development, governance reform, and caring for the elderly.

Alison Kadlec is senior vice president for public engagement and director of the Center for Advances in Public Engagement (CAPE) at Public Agenda. She is active in the design, implementation, and evaluation of public engagement and research projects across the country. A political theorist by training, she is the author of *Dewey's Critical Pragmatism*.

Robert J. Kingston is a senior associate of the Kettering Foundation. He grew up in England, was educated at Oxford, and first came to this country (of which he is now a citizen) as a professor of Shakespeare at the University of Michigan. A former president of the College Board, Kingston served as deputy chairman of the National Endowment for the Humanities in the Nixon, Ford, and Carter administrations and was executive director of Public Agenda in its formative years. At Kettering, Kingston is editor of the *Kettering Review* and executive producer of the annual television program *A Public Voice*; assists in the developing of collaborative projects with other organizations—like the international "Deliberative Democracy Workshops" and the "National Issues Convention" (with MacNeil/Lehrer Productions and the Center for Deliberative Democracy at Stanford); and has contributed to the planning of virtually all the foundation's operating programs.

Keith Melville is a sociologist and professor who has taught college- and graduate-level programs for the past thirty years. Trained as a PhD sociologist at Columbia University, he has held faculty positions at the City University of New York and the Fielding Graduate University, one of the first and most respected distance learning programs for midcareer doctoral students. He also worked in the White House (1978–1981) as senior writer for the President's Commission for a National Agenda, and subsequently was senior vice president of Public Agenda, where he was a co-creator of the National Issues Forums, the largest national network of community forums about public issues today.

Steven A. Rosell is president and co-founder of Viewpoint Learning, Inc., where he leads the development of its innovative dialogue-based techniques and their application in both business and the public sector.

Daniel Yankelovich is chairman and co-founder of both Public Agenda and Viewpoint Learning, Inc. He has spent more than forty years monitoring social change and public opinion in America. He initiated the *New York Times*/Yankelovich Poll and founded both DYG, Inc., a firm that tracks social and market trends, and the market research firm of Yankelovich, Skelly, and White (now Yankelovich Partners). Yankelovich is the author of twelve books, including *Coming to Public Judgment: Making Democracy Work in a Complex World* (1991).

Index

Page numbers in boldface refer to figures and tables.